Steven K. Mittwede

Jesus' Authority in Markan Perspective

Steven K. Mittwede

Jesus' Authority in Markan Perspective

Scope and Missiological Implications

Fromm Verlag

Imprint

Bibliographic information published by the Deutsche Nationalbibliothek: The Deutsche Nationalbibliothek lists this publication in the Deutsche Nationalbibliografie; detailed bibliographic data are available in the Internet at http://dnb.d-nb.de.

Publisher:
Fromm Verlag is an imprint of the publishing house
VDM Publishing House Ltd.,17 Rue Meldrum, Beau Bassin,1713-01 Mauritius
Website: www.frommverlag.de
Email: info@frommverlag.de

Published in 2011

Printed in: U.S.A., U.K., Germany. This book was not produced in Mauritius.

ISBN: 978-3-8416-0021-9

CONTENTS

ABBREVIATIONS

Periodicals

Bib *Biblica*

BSac *Bibliotheca Sacra*

CBQ *Catholic Biblical Quarterly*

ChrCent *Christian Century*

EMQ *Evangelical Missions Quarterly*

EvQ *Evangelical Quarterly*

ExpTim *Expository Times*

Int *Interpretation*

JBL *Journal of Biblical Literature*

JETS *Journal of the Evangelical Theological Society*

JSNT *Journal for the Study of the New Testament*

JTS *Journal of Theological Studies*

NTS *New Testament Studies*

NovT *Novum Testamentum*

RevExp *Review and Expositor*

SBET *Scottish Bulletin of Evangelical Theology*

WTJ *Westminster Theological Journal*

ZNW *Zeitschrift für die neutestamentliche Wissenschaft*

Reference Works

BAGD *Bauer, Arndt, Gingrich & Danker* (Greek-English Lexicon)

EDNT *Exegetical Dictionary of the New Testament*

TDNT *Theological Dictionary of the New Testament*

Publishers

BOT Banner of Truth Trust

CFP Christian Focus Publications

CUP Cambridge University Press

IVP Inter-Varsity Press

OUP Oxford University Press

SAP Sheffield Academic Press

UNC University of North Carolina Press

WJK Westminster John Knox Press

INTRODUCTION

A traditional Reformed reading of certain texts of the New Testament indicates that the salvation of an individual is only by the gracious, sovereign work of God (e.g., Saul in Acts 9; also, see Rom. 8:11; Eph. 2:1-10). Unless the Holy Spirit quickens the heart of a man*, that man will not respond in faith to God's free offer of salvation, for no one naturally seeks after God (Rom. 3:11).

Nevertheless, some have proposed the use of *redemptive analogies* as a means of bridging cultural barriers and thus facilitating the explanation of the Gospel in different cultural contexts.[1] When done within the bounds of hermeneutical propriety, a redemptive analogy can be a powerful means of kindling an understanding of the Gospel among individuals of a target people group.

A danger is assuming that when such a redemptive analogy is used, it will necessarily lead to the salvation of all with whom it is shared, as if salvation can be reduced to an "If...then..." formula, or a sort of incantation.

In spite of this caveat, cross-cultural ministers would be delinquent to neglect the use of a possibly powerful redemptive analogy when it is at their disposal. However, we should ask this question: Is there a biblical basis for redemptive analogies? It would seem that Paul's reference to the unknown god of the Athenians in his "Areopagitica" in Acts 17 was an attempt to link an element of Athenian culture to the truth of the gospel of Jesus Christ. Moreover, Paul quoted two ancient Greek poets in order to impart a sense of relevance to what he communicated in that discourse. These bridges were at least partially effective in that some Athenians believed (Acts 17:34).

---

* Herein, traditional masculine forms are used generically to refer to any human being or individual. No connotation of male superiority or domination is intended.

[1] E.g., Don Richardson, *Peace Child* (Glendale, California: G/L Regal, 1974).

Although a much abused passage – and the interpretational underpinning for much missiological error[2], under the rubric of contextualisation – the gospel minister should be able to appeal appropriately to the teaching of 1 Cor. 9:22b, the intent of which the New Living Translation captures well: *Yes, I try to find common ground with everyone so that I might bring them to Christ.* The possibility of a lost soul coming into God's family should be amongst our highest values, demanding that we be willing – for the sake of the gospel – to be labelled as subversives, derided as "seedpickers", and prepared thoroughly as scholars.[3]

The foundational principal behind the present work is that the best missiologists are faithful, careful theologians.[4] Good missiology issues from good theology. Thus, our first commitment must be to "doing theology" within the biblically prescribed guidelines. Our expectation should be that these guidelines can be apprehended through focused study of the Bible with an eye to grasping both its unchanging message and also insights for its teaching and application in our own and other cultures.

A study of the fabric of the Mark's gospel indicates that the issue of authority is part of the warp and woof of that account of Jesus' life and ministry. In so far as authority also plays a powerful role in Turkish society – the present writer's home for the past 20 years – it seems prudent to explore the possibility that Jesus' authority may constitute a bridge from the gospel account to Turkish culture, facilitating the explanation of who Jesus is, what his "claims" are, and why he should matter to a people group that has been historically resistant to the Christian message. In order to evaluate

---

[2] E.g., John Speers has suggested that cross-cultural ministers to Muslims should keep the Muslim fast in an effort to identify more fully with their target audience. See "Ramadan: Should Missionaries keep the Muslim fast?" *EMQ* 27/4 (1991): 356-359. Obviously, there is a biblical precedent for fasting, but purposely fasting at Ramadan sends a wrong and deceptive message to our Muslim friends.

[3] Steven K. Mittwede, "Evangelism at Athens: Paul's Adaptability," *Reformation Today* 161 (1998): 15-18.

the plausibility of this proposal, it is necessary that significant elements of the christological content of the Markan account be surveyed and evaluated, in particular the design of Mark's gospel and the significance of the christological titles he uses, as well as the scope and implications of Jesus' authority – implicit and explicit – as presented therein.

[4] This is true so long as the flexibility and adaptability that characterises the most capable

1. THE CHALLENGE OF CONTEXTUALISATION AND THE PROMISE OF REDEMPTIVE ANALOGIES

Contextualisation

Over the past three decades, the issue of contextualisation has come to occupy centre stage in many missiological debates. Although the term itself was only coined early in 1972,[5] the concept is age-old and has been the concern of cross-cultural communicators from biblical times.[6]

Unfortunately, there is no consensus concerning what the term actually means. Certainly it is used in a variety of ways. Some workers suggest that the neologism *contextualisation* is unnecessary in that it is really no different than the well-worn term *indigenisation*.[7] However, as Bruce Nicholls notes, "the concerns of the advocates of contextualization are valid."[8] He goes on to point out that "Contextualization takes seriously the contemporary factors in cultural change."[9] In other words, it is claimed that contextualisation recognises and takes into account the dynamism of culture rather than focusing only on traditional cultural values. In any case, "the contextualizing of the gospel...cannot be separated from the work of evangelism and the indigenizing of the church."[10]

The point remains, however, that missiologists define contextualisation in various ways. Hesselgrave and Rommen expound three chief categories or types of contextualisation, namely, apostolic, prophetic and syncretistic.[11]

---

missiologists/missionaries does not translate into sloppy, haphazard theologising.

[5] Bruce J. Nicholls, *Contextualization* (Downers Grove: IVP, 1978), 21, and David J. Hesselgrave and Edward Rommen, *Contextualization: Meanings, Methods, and Models* (Grand Rapids: Baker, 1989), 28-32.

[6] Hesselgrave and Rommen, ibid., 3-26.

[7] E.g., James O. Buswell, whose position is explained by Nicholls, op. cit., 21.

[8] Ibid., 21.

[9] Ibid., 22.

[10] Ibid., 23.

[11] Op. cit., 148-151.

The emphasis in apostolic contextualisation is on contextualising the apostolic faith "to the people of a respondent culture in such a way as to preserve as much of its original meaning and relevance as possible."[12] The following definition by Bruce Nicholls, one of those who espouses this sort of contextualisation, captures well the perspective:

> the translation of the unchanging content of the Gospel of the Kingdom into verbal form meaningful to the peoples in their separate cultures and within their particular existential situation.[13]

The theological commitments of the proponents of contextualisation, thus defined, are obvious. The content of the Gospel is not negotiable, nor is its meaning derived from context; however, its meaning *is* communicated in a way that it is truly understandable by the target people.

Prophetic contextualisation differs from the apostolic type in its focus on the communicator determining what God is doing and saying in a newly entered culture, and then speaking and working for the needed change.[14] In this type of contextualisation, the emphasis is typically more on context than on content *per se*, as in many examples of liberation theology.

In syncretistic contextualisation, an effort is made to move toward truth via accommodation of various cultures and belief systems, seeking to identify and adopt the best of each.[15] Obviously, in the contextualisation continuum, the syncretistic type strongly emphasises the human elements in revelation whereas the apostolic type strongly emphasises the supracultural or divine elements in biblical revelation.[16] Apostolic contextualisation thus reflects the traditional evangelical approach toward Scripture.

---

[12] Ibid., 149.
[13] Quoted in Hesselgrave and Rommen, ibid., 149.
[14] Ibid., 150.
[15] Hesselgrave and Rommen, op. cit., 151.
[16] Ibid.

In the present work, the apostolic type of contextualisation is embraced, yet it must be stressed that this position does not grant the cross-cultural communicator licence to ignore cultural mores. Rather, it recognises that – if the cross-cultural minister of the Good News is to be effective – he must be not only a student of the Bible, but also of the target culture. Thus, to truly communicate cross-culturally, he must accurately understand the message of Scripture, namely God's self-revelation and His plan of redemption, *and* the nuances of language, values, beliefs, customs and practices, and social relationships in the culture in which he ministers.

Redemptive Analogies

One aspect of contextualisation that may hold unusual promise for the cross-cultural minister is the *redemptive analogy*. Don Richardson calls redemptive analogies "God's keys to man's cultures", indicating that these are the "New Testament-approved approach to cross-cultural evangelism."[17] In Richardson's own experience with the headhunting, cannibalistic Sawi people of Papua New Guinea, he discovered that a local legend told of a "peace child", a baby entrusted by one tribe to an enemy tribe, who would bring an end to the hostilities between estranged tribes – a sort of treachery-ending détente. He understood this legend to be a God-implanted picture of God's own Peace Child, Jesus Christ, and thus was able to use the Sawi legend to explain the Good News of alienation-ending salvation in Christ (e.g., 2 Cor. 5:18-19; Eph. 2, esp.13-16).

Richardson surmises "that God...providentially plants Christ-foreshadowing elements in other cultures as well", and notes that redemptive analogies "may be either *general* to many cultures or *special* to one culture." [18] Further, he suggests that redemptive

---

[17] Op. cit., 288.

[18] "Redemptive Analogies," in *Evangelical Dictionary of World Missions*, eds. A. Scott Moreau, Harold Netland and Charles Van Engen (Grand Rapids: Baker, 2000), 812.

analogies are "evidence that God has been making a positive communication through general revelation."[19]

Others have made similar proposals. Gerald McDermott evaluates the biblical evidence for revelation in other religions, and concludes that indeed "the Bible contains hints and suggestions that God has given knowledge of Himself to people and traditions outside the Hebrew and Christian traditions."[20] He admits that the evidence is "neither overwhelming nor crystal clear", but *is* sufficient to make a claim that this proposal is "biblically *plausible*", and stresses that such knowledge is not salvific.[21]

Terrance Tiessen – who roundly rejects proposals that the scriptures of other religions are divine revelation, and that the founders or leading teachers of other religions should be called "prophets" in the line of divinely authoritative messengers within Israel – sets forth this cogent thesis:

> In God's gracious providence, he may have caused or allowed ideas to emerge within a religious context that provide a bridge or stepping stone toward the gospel, thereby facilitating communication of the gospel to those people and becoming an instrument of the Spirit of God in eliciting faith in Christ.[22]

Similarly, McDermott claims there are, in the religions, scattered promises of God in Christ that the triune God has planted there as "revealed types".[23]

Thus, such bridges might be construed as evidence of God's common grace which works hand in hand with God's special, saving grace to accomplish God's redemptive purposes in the world. However, it must be emphasised that there is no Christless grace. All grace, special *and* common, is mediated by Christ.[24]

---

[19] Ibid., 813.
[20] *Can Evangelicals Learn from World Religions?* (Downers Grove: IVP, 2000), 73.
[21] Ibid., 74.
[22] *Who Can be Saved?* (Downers Grove: IVP, 2004), 358.
[23] Op. cit., 114.
[24] E.g., see W.C. Campbell-Jack, "Common Grace and Eschatology," *SBET* 7/2 (1989): 109-110. Note also that certain scriptural texts clearly indicate that God's redemptive work in Christ was accomplished before the foundation of the world (e.g., Eph. 1:4; 1 Pet. 1:20; Rev. 17:8).

Other redemptive analogies have been recognised in the culture of the Dinka people of Sudan. Joy Anderson reports that "the Dinka culture displays many such bridges to the gospel."[25] For example, in so far as the Dinka believe that cattle protect them from evil, and their generic term for sacrifice is "ox", cross-cultural ministers there can refer to the perfect sacrifice, Jesus, as the "Ox of God".[26] Anderson notes: "God has allowed each culture to develop in a way that prepares people of that culture for the gospel."[27]

Indeed, it seems that redemptive analogies might await discovery and application in a multitude of cultural contexts. Because of a wideness in God's mercy and grace, we can expect that He has providentially allowed cultures to develop in such a way as to contain "bridging" elements for use by Christ's ambassadors.

A biblical example of bridge-building contextualisation, already referred to above, is Paul on Mars Hill in Acts 17. In line with apostolic contextualisation as described above, John Appleby notes that Paul built bridges with great care, such that "in no way did he so modify the gospel as to rob it of its truth and its challenge."[28] He continues:

> Paul [at Athens]...did not express the gospel in Old Testament religious patterns, because his hearers would not have known what he was talking about if he had. The truths he presented *were* thoroughly biblical truths, yet were expressed within the limits of Athenian thought-patterns. Similarly, the words we use when we speak to the biblically illiterate need to be words *they* will understand.[29]

Possible Pitfalls

A great temptation in cross-cultural ministry, especially in resistant contexts, is to assume that there is "a golden key that can

---

[25] "Behold the Ox of God?" *EMQ* 34/3 (1998): 316.

[26] Ibid., 316-317.

[27] Ibid., 320.

[28] "Paul on Mars Hill: Our Role-Model for Evangelising People Around Us Today? *Foundations* (Spring 2004): 24.

[29] Ibid., 26.

miraculously unlock the stubborn tightly closed door."[30] In fact, a perceived redemptive analogy can wrongly be counted a "magic wand" that will guarantee success. Alternatively, the cross-cultural minister may so want success, namely faith commitments from nationals in his target group, that he is willing to do *anything*; thus, he may jump into the sin of expediency – the end justifies the means.[31]

As Michael Wakely points out, every ministry "key" should be subjected to a number of preliminary tests. *First,* is this key true? Does it at least conform to and, preferably, arise from Holy Scripture?[32] Each worker must ask himself if he is remaining true to his theological commitments, regardless of how difficult the task may seem. *Second,* does the end justify the means?[33] I submit that God has given at least a general framework of normative principles for use in cross-cultural ministry. If this is the case, this framework[34] constitutes the "means" that we should employ in our ministry. The end is for God to determine, and the fruit belongs to the Holy Spirit. Therefore, although we may be passionately concerned about the end, our focus must be upon faithful adherence to the divinely revealed or allowed means. If the end becomes our focus, we will almost certainly slide into syncretism, having lost our grip on the unchanging content of the biblical message.[35] *Third,* there are keys that appear to have fit

---

[30] Mike Wakely, "The Search for the Golden Key," *EMQ* 40/1 (2004): 12.

[31] Wakely, ibid., 15, notes: "...there is a temptation for missionaries to become pragmatic theologians in our search for successful methods." As an example, Wakely quotes well-known missiologist C. Peter Wagner who admits that he has "a bias towards theories that work."

[32] Ibid., 14. In the same vein, Gary Corwin comments that, in our heartfelt desire to reach the lost, we sometimes embrace a warped perspective "that confuses eternal truths for issues of cultural contextualization." ("Reaching the Resistant," *EMQ* 34/2 (1998): 145).

[33] Ibid., 15.

[34] However, admittedly there are many ideas or practices that may be permissible but concerning which Scripture is silent or neutral.

[35] Phil Parshall ("Danger! New Directions in Contextualization," *EMQ* 34/4 (1998)) and Scott Woods ("Biblical Look at C5 Muslim Evangelism," *EMQ* 39/2 (2003)) warn against exactly this. They note that many practitioners of so-called "C5" Muslim evangelism are crossing the line into syncretism. C5 refers to a level of contextualisation wherein some missionaries "become Muslims" to reach Muslims for Christ, and where Christ-centered communities are made up of "Messianic Muslim" believers who remain legally and socially within the community of Islam (see Parshall with sidebar by John Travis, 408-412). Parshall (410) urges C5 cross-cultural ministers to "more fully consider both the Islamic charge of deception as well as the long-term consequences of their actions." Similarly,

certain rusty locks.[36] Some ministry keys will not fit the lock we are trying to open; nevertheless, what can we learn from these keys that may be useful in our own ministry contexts? Here, the critical issue is that cross-cultural workers maintain a learner's stance, always searching for opportunities and methods consonant with biblical guidelines.

Wood notes "that there is a vast difference between being culturally relevant and theologically accommodating" (191), and asks "How far is too far in contextualization?" (189).

[36] Ibid., 15.

2. THE CASE OF *ÜSTATLIK* AND RELATED CONCEPTS IN TURKISH CULTURE

What should be clear from the above discussion is that, while certainly the Good News should be communicated transculturally in a way that is both true to the biblical deposit and also sensitive to the receptor culture, it is not uncommon for well-meaning ministers to fall into syncretistic error. One aspect of contextualisation, namely the recognition and application of redemptive analogies, holds especial promise, though not without potential dangers – such as a starry-eyed search for a "golden key".

These caveats notwithstanding, an intimate understanding of Scripture, properly interpreted, should direct the efforts of cross-cultural ministers. Thus, the priority in sound missiology must be sound theology, from which will issue – by God's gracious work through the Holy Spirit – a circumspect, properly balanced evangelistic method.

Sociological Insights

Over the course of 20 years of life and work in Turkey, it has become clear to me that Turks generally hold in high esteem people in authority or of rank. Traditionally, most people who enter the workforce want to enter positions that are respected or esteemed because of the authority held by ones in these offices.[37] Accordingly, various "experts" and "masters"[38], master craftsmen, military and political leaders, high-level bureaucrats, teachers, and religious leaders are highly regarded. Not surprisingly, a multitude of special

[37] However, there is an ever-increasing rush towards medicine, law and engineering; this trend is largely motivated more by desire for material gain and the comfort that it brings than for desire for the honour that comes with other, more traditional, positions of authority.

[38] Including, but not limited to various artists (musicians, artists, literary figures, etc.) and scientists.

titles are used the Turkish language, such as *ağa, bey, efendi, hoca, paşa, şeyh, usta,* and *üstat.*[39]

In order to test my perceptions in this regard, an informal survey, comprising four questions, was prepared in order to gain insights from a group[40] of unscientifically selected Turkish nationals concerning their understanding of titles/positions of authority in Turkish society. Translated, the four survey questions – referring to the following four titles (concepts) – are:

ÜSTAT (LIK) *USTA (LIK)* *HOCA (LIK)* *YETKİLİ KİŞİ*

1) *Without referring to a dictionary or any other reference work, write an explanatory or descriptive definition for each of the above four words.*
2) *In your opinion, is there any conceptual relationship among these words? If so, what?*
3) *When you hear or read these words, what sort of feelings do they awaken in you or impressions do they leave upon you? Positive or negative? Why?*
4) *Are these concepts important or not for Turkish society? Why?*

---

[39] Turkish translations of these titles are as follows: *ağa* = lord, master, or local large landowner; *bey* = gentleman, sir, also prince, ruler chieftain, chief, master; *efendi* = gentleman, master, or historically a title given to literate people, members of the clergy, Ottoman princes and army officers up to major; *hoca* = Muslim preacher, also teacher, instructor; *paşa* = admiral, general, or historically (in Ottoman times) a title given to high-ranking civil servants or soldiers; *şeyh* = head of a group of dervishes or other religious order (or, *de facto*, of an associated trade guild), or Arab tribal head (sheikh); *usta* = master (of a trade or craft), or master workman or craftsman, expert; *üstat* = master, recognised expert or authority, or savant, or virtuoso. Another modern term in general use is *yetkili kişi* = authorised, warranted (responsible) or competent person. From *Çağdaş Türkçe-İngilizce Redhouse Sözlüğü* [Redhouse Contemporary Turkish-English Dictionary] (İstanbul: Redhouse Yayınevi, 1983).

[40] The survey was completed by thirty-eight ethnic Turks, all above age 17. The respondents all live in cities or towns of central Anatolia, Turkey: six in Ankara (pop. ~3,500,000); twenty five in Avanos, Nevşehir Province (pop. ~13,000); and seven in Konya (pop. ~812,000) (these figures reflect 2004 estimates).

The titles-survey results show no perceptible variation among the three populations centers in which the respondents live. That is, the answers do not seem to vary on the basis of population size.[41]

All but three of the respondents considered the titles to be *positive* terms, and held these concepts or titles to be *important* or very important in Turkish society. Likewise, all but four of the respondents[42] perceived a conceptual relationship among these titles, although some correctly noted that "authorised person" differs from the other three titles.

On the other hand, none of the respondents mentioned the "authority connection" *per se*; rather, persons with these titles were considered to have *superior knowledge, skills, rank or influence*, or to be *experts* in their field. One respondent reported that the conceptual thread that binds the titles is *uniqueness*; another mentioned the idea of *hierarchy*, and two saw *responsibility* as a common thread. Several respondents noted that all of the concepts possess an *educational/ instructional* meaning.

Generally speaking, all respondents were able to give acceptable definitions for the four titles/concepts. Somewhat unexpectedly for the present researcher, 45% of the respondents communicated that the title *üstat* is the loftiest of these titles[43]; that is, one who is called *üstat* deserves the highest respect because of his superior knowledge, ability and/or experience. Thus, an *üstat* is widely considered to be at the pinnacle of his field.

[41] Admittedly, all three of these "outlier" responses came from the town of Avanos, but these respondents *may* be explainable as societally marginalised or politically extreme individuals.

[42] The same three respondents differed from the rest of the sample population on this question (2) as on questions 3 and 4. One respondent left question 2 blank.

[43] It is noteworthy that one of the two modern Turkish translations of the New Testament (Turkish Bible Society, 1999) has Jesus addressed as *üstat* in a number of places in Luke's gospel: e.g., 5:5, 8:24, 8:45, 9:33, 9:49, 17:13; elsewhere, the more typical *efendi* is used. In that translation, *üstat* is used to translate the Greek ἐπιστάτης and *efendi* the Greek χύριος.

Leadership and Authority in Turkish Islam

Turkey is a secular republic with parliamentary democracy; thus, it is unlike neighbouring Iran and wealthy Saudi Arabia in that Islamic law (*şeriat*) is not the basis of the legal system. However, the vast majority of Turks, more than 99% of the populace of 77 million, *are* legally and socially Muslims, even if many are only nominally so. There are of course, devout, orthodox or "traditional" Muslims in Turkey; in fact, their number seems to be on the rise if the almost unprecedented success of the Islamist Justice and Development Party (A*K PARTİ*) in the last two general elections, and the marked increase in attendance at Friday (*Cuma*) noon prayers over the last decade, are reliable indicators. Nevertheless, Islam in Turkey does not play as prominent a role in public life as it does elsewhere in the Middle East.

However, there *is* compulsory religious education in public schools, and the government has a large and powerful division attached directly to the office of the Prime Minister, the Department of Religious Affairs, which oversees and supports Turkey's Sunni mosques.[44] In 1990, the budgetary allowance for this department increased by 237 percent, and its budget was then superior to nine full ministries.[45] Other Turkish government ministries, including tourism and culture, also "affirm" this thoroughly Muslim social milieu by encouraging faith tourism[46] and some religious publishing, respectively. For example, a classic text on Islam recently re-published by the Turkish Ministry of Culture claims this:

> in the religion of Islam there are no such things as a representative of God (Allah) or a class of clerics; there is no guide other than the Qur'an, and no vehicle other than the Prophet (Muhammad).[47]

---

[44] Philip Robins, *Turkey and the Middle East* (London: Pinter/RIIA, 1991): 40.

[45] Ibid., 40.

[46] Admittedly, many of the most-visited sites are "Christian" but, of course, personages such as Abraham and Jesus are claimed as prophets of Islam, so many "Christian" sites are visited by Turks as well as by foreign tourists. In fact, the traditional house of Mary, Jesus' mother, near the ruins of Ephesus, is flooded by Turkish tourists as a site of minor pilgrimage.

[47] Yusuf Ziya Yörükhân, *Müslümanlık ve Kur'an-ı Kerim'den Âyetlerle İslâm Esasları* (Ankara: Turkish Ministry of Culture, 2002), 163.

The emphasis in the context is that there is no pope-like figure, there are no priests, and no mediators between the worshipper and God.

Similarly, Bernard Lewis, Princeton expert on the Middle East and especially on modern Turkey, notes that in classical Islam, "there are no lords spiritual" and no hierarchy.[48] Thus, it would seem that the edifice of orthodox Islam recognises no sort of human authority within its walls.

In stark contrast to this situation is that reported from within the *tarikat* system of Turkey. A *tarikat*[49] is a religious order or brotherhood, often mystical, best known in reference to Sufi (dervish) sects.[50] Although these orders were outlawed at one time for fear that they were seedbeds of subversion[51], today membership in these orders across Turkey is growing and influential.[52]

Each *tarikat* "is centered on a particular charismatic individual, or master."[53] These leaders are regarded so highly that it is believed that "Truthful and saving knowledge cannot come from books...but only through the proper person, the master."[54] Thus, these orders place great emphasis on the master as the source of learning.

---

[48] *What Went Wrong?* (London: Weidenfeld & Nicolson, 2002), 100. Lewis goes further with this explanation: "One may even say that there is no orthodoxy or heresy, if one understand these terms in the Christian sense, as correct or incorrect belief defined as such by duly constituted religious authority. *There has never been any such authority in Islam, and consequently no such definition.*" [emphasis added].

[49] This word, derived from Arabic, literally means "path".

[50] Adil Özdemir and Kenneth Frank, *Visible Islam in Modern Turkey* (Basingstoke: Macmillan, 2000), 66.

[51] Özdemir and Frank emphasise that these orders "are neither extremist cults nor ascetic movements." Ibid.

[52] Ibid., 65. These authors write: "Not every Muslim in Turkey belongs to a religious order. But many do, and their activities are numerous and growing. They are playing a significant role in the continuing transformation of the country."

[53] Ibid., 66.

Accordingly,

> the ideal is that the new disciple places his or her life in the hands of the master and establishes a relationship of perfect obedience...Only then can the saving, truthful knowledge flow into the disciple. The premium is on the submission of the individual's will to that of the master...[55]

What is clear from the foregoing is that, although human religious hierarchy is not an element of traditional, orthodox Islam, there is a strong commitment and devotion to authoritative leaders within the religious orders of Turkey. Consequently, it seems appropriate to conclude that – based upon sociological observations and the disciple-master relationship within the not-insignificant *tarikat* system of Turkey – most Turks not only revere strong leaders or authority figures but also desire them, willingly placing themselves under the guidance of such authorities.

---

[54] Ibid., 67.

[55] Ibid. Interestingly, when a new disciple (*mürit*) placed himself under the care and direction of his master (*mürşit* or *şeyh*), "he was embarking on a process which sufis began to describe as a 'second birth'", and the master was "viewed as a metaphorical father (sometimes mother), a person through whom God works to bring humanity to true maturity." Yaşar Nuri Öztürk, *The Eye of the Heart* (İstanbul: Redhouse, 1988), 21-22. The parallels between these ideas and some Christian doctrines are obvious.

3. THE SCOPE OF JESUS' AUTHORITY IN MARK'S GOSPEL

We have established that the important realm of contextualisation presents a multitude of challenges, especially for ministry in resistant contexts. Conversely, certain types of contextualisation – in our discussion, redemptive analogies – hold promise of great fruitfulness. In that traditionally resistant Turkish culture grants a special place to authoritative leaders, it is proposed that Jesus' authority, as recorded in Mark's gospel, may constitute a bridge to Turkish culture which will facilitate Turkish Muslims' understanding of Jesus' person and work, such that Jesus may be recognised as the *üstat* of the spiritual realm.

Rationale for choosing Mark

Following the majority of recent scholars, I accept the priority of Mark among the Synoptic gospels. In his recent commentary, James Edwards summarises well the argument set forth in the first half of the nineteenth century for Markan priority and the consequent proliferation of Markan studies.[56] Rather than being seen as a slavish copier of Matthew, Mark's gospel is widely recognised as the earliest gospel and, thus, the most "primitive" account of Jesus' life and work. Furthermore, Edwards holds that "Mark was a skilled literary artist and theologian" rather than the earlier-held view that Mark was "a clumsy and artless writer."[57] Elsewhere Edwards makes a strong case for convergence of Mark's "literary and theological craftsmanship" in his so-called "sandwich technique"[58], the "breaking up of a story or

[56] *The Gospel according to Mark* (Grand Rapids: Eerdmans, 2002): 2-3. So, for example, A. T. Robertson, *Studies in Mark's Gospel* (Nashville: Broadman, 1958), 15-16; Paul J. Achtemeier, *Mark* (Philadelphia: Fortress, 1986), 6-7; R. T. France, *Divine Government* (London: SPCK, 1990), 4; James Brooks, *Mark* (Nashville: Broadman, 1991), 23-25.

[57] Ibid., 3.

[58] "Markan Sandwiches: The Significance of Interpolations in Markan Narratives," *NovT* 31/3 (1989), 216.

pericope by inserting a second, seemingly unrelated, story into the middle of it."[59] Mark uses this technique on nine occasions "in order to underscore the major motifs of his Gospel", and shows great subtlety and sophistication, either by illustrating an ideal (e.g. faith, in 5:21-43) or by creating a contrast "between the ways of God and the ways of humanity."[60]

In addition to the supposed priority of Mark's gospel, another key reason for choosing his account is its fast pace. For the uninitiated, the action of Mark's account is often preferable to the more teaching-heavy accounts of Matthew, Luke and John. Ralph Martin's perspectives capture well the attractiveness of Mark's account:

> ...its language is clear, its narrative of Jesus' life is swift-flowing and entertaining, and its appeal to the non-theological mind is direct...Mark's Gospel is full of activity, rich in dramatic quality, and centred on a heroic figure whose master-mind controls the movement of the plot. Talking is not much in his line (in this gospel); and he strides across the chapters with a singleness of purpose and a magnetic appeal to others which identifies him as a Leader with obvious charisma.[61]

Therefore, because it is considered "primitive" Christian proclamation, and also is clear and swift-flowing in its presentation, Mark's gospel is ideal for the purposes of the present study. Furthermore, as will be discussed in more detail below, many scholars recognise the importance of Jesus' authority in Mark's theological programme.

The Meaning of ἐξουσία

The Greek word for authority is ἐξουσία. This term is used in the Septuagint to mean "right, authority, permission or freedom in the legal or political sense, and it is then used for the right or permission given by God", and in the New Testament (NT) it denotes "the power of God in nature and the spiritual world" and "especially the power or

[59] Ibid., 193.

[60] Ibid., 216. See also the discussion of this technique by Anne Dawson, *Freedom as Liberating Power* (Göttingen: Vandenhoeck & Ruprecht, 2000), 156-157, 167, 180.

freedom which is given to Jesus, and by Him to His disciples."[62] Almost every explanation of the NT meaning of ἐξουσία marries the concept of freedom to act to a concurrent power to "back up" or support that freedom. It is unlike δύναμις, which means simply "power", and implies more the innate or inherent ability to act.[63] Foerster notes three "foundations" upon which ἐξουσία in the NT thought-world rests: 1) power of decision; 2) its activity in a legally order whole; and 3) its continuous exercise, especially in the freedom given to the community.[64] All of these aspects are subsumed under "the lordship of God in a fallen world where nothing takes place apart from His ἐξουσία or authority."[65] In particular, this term is important in understanding the Jesus' person and work. Denoted is Jesus' "divinely given power and authority to act."[66] As we will see below, Jesus' authority was either explicitly or implicitly expressed in multifarious ways and contexts all through Mark's account.

Ingo Broer reports that ἐξουσία is used in the NT 102 times, with the most occurrences in Revelation (21) and Luke (16).[67] The term occurs nine times in Mark's gospel. Citing the range of meaning assigned by *BAGD* – namely 1) freedom, right; 2) ability, power; and 3) authority, warrant – Broer notes that "*these meanings are fluid* (emphasis added) because right and authority cross over to each other, authority presupposes power/ability...and the first meaning encompasses the third."[68] Yet, although fluid, proper use of the term

---

[61] *Mark: Evangelist and Theologian* (Grand Rapids: Zondervan, 1973 [1972]), 11.

[62] Werner Foerster, "ἐξουσία," *TDNT*, 2:564-565. Also used in the Septuagint as the "unrestricted sovereignty of God." I. Broer, "ἐξουσία," *EDNT*, 2:10.

[63] Norval Geldenhuys, *Supreme Authority* (London: Marshall, Morgan & Scott, 1953), 15.

[64] Op. cit., 566. Richard Dillon also discusses the meaning of ἐξουσία, especially relative to δύναμις; they are not the same – the distinction between them is sometimes indistinct – but it approximates the difference between right and ability. Thus, ἐξουσία carries the idea of *legitimacy*, denoting "the right to act and the accorded possibility of action; it connotes entitlement, permission, commission...[and] draws surprisingly close to *freedom*." See his "'As One Having Authority' (Mark 1:22): The Controversial Distinction of Jesus' Teaching," *CBQ* 57/1 (1995): 97-98.

[65] Ibid., 566.

[66] Ibid., 568. Foerster continues: "If He is the Son, this authority is not a restricted commission. It is His own rule in free agreement with the Father."

[67] Op. cit.

[68] Ibid.

must appreciate and accept the fullness of the interrelationship of these meanings. Warrant without power or ability is frustratingly hollow and really no warrant at all, exercise of power without legitimate warrant is tyranny at worst or simple bullying at best, and exercise of power without right is either lawlessness or impersonation. When properly understood and expressed, true ἐξουσία is winsome and almost magnetic in its attraction. As Nicholas Sagovsky points out, "authority *is* a form of power" (emphasis added), moderated by responsibility."[69] Thus, "it may be exercised in ways that make for freedom or restraint."[70]

Of the usage of ἐξουσία in Mark 1:22, 27, Daube profoundly limits the import of Jesus' authority by arguing at length that authority here refers to "rabbinic authority", as conferred through special ordination by one already authorised.[71] However, Argyle and Westerholm have effectively countered Daube's conclusion: the former notes that Mark 1:22 certainly does not establish this meaning, and the latter that "authority in this period was not attached to a formal act of ordination" and that, in any case, ordination never granted licence to ignore or violate the religious laws, which Jesus was clearly considered by the Jewish leaders to have done.[72]

The Magnitude of Jesus' ἐξουσία

People are amazed and drawn toward proper authority, but are also regularly fooled because they fail to recognise when authority is not fully orbed. A leader in government or commerce, for instance, may have warrant by reason of office, but may either misuse his power or lack the moral authority to have his directives enforced. At times, authority is usurped – or thought to be so – leading to conflict.

---

[69] "Lifelines: Church and Authority," *Anvil* 14/3 (1997): 207.

[70] Ibid.

[71] "ἐξουσία in Mark 1 22 and 27," *JTS* 39 (1938): 45-59.

[72] A. W. Argyle, "The Meaning of ἐξουσία in Mark 1:22,27," *ExpTim* 80 (1969): 343; Stephen Westerholm, *Jesus and Scribal Authority* (Coniectanea Biblica, NT Series 10). Lund: CWK Gleerup, 1978.

Sometimes, authority is fully orbed and completely legitimate yet, because of human sin and rebelliousness, it is spurned or ignored.

The authority of Jesus, the quintessential leader[73], is expressed or implied throughout Mark's gospel. In places his authority is simply reported, elsewhere it is claimed and, yet in other places, it is practically demonstrated or proven. Conversely, it is - in some instances - challenged or rejected by his opponents.

This quality of Jesus' life and work is so prominent in Mark's account that some theologians have suggested that it is one of the predominant, fundamental christological aspects of this gospel.[74] James Edwards asserts Jesus' ἐξουσία[75] is "the one characteristic that left the most lasting impression on his followers and caused the greatest offense to his opponents".[76] Further, Edwards suggests that "the essential and distinctive characteristic of Jesus" is his ἐξουσία.[77]

Morna Hooker notes Mark's unpolished style but admits that his arrangement of material is sophisticated.[78] In particular, the first eight chapters of Mark's gospel are replete with explicit and implicit expressions of Jesus' authority, as Hooker makes clear in her succinct exposition of those texts.[79] Consequently, it is wise to conclude that this emphasis is meant to lay a foundation for the remainder of Mark's

---

[73] Karl Heim, *Jesus the Lord* (Edinburgh: Oliver and Boyd, 1959), closely argues the philosophical and theological basis for, and the practical necessity and uniqueness of, Jesus' leadership.

[74] E.g., Demetrios Trakatellis, in his compelling book, *Authority and Passion* (Brookline, Massachusetts: Holy Cross Orthodox Press, 1987), asserts that a "Christology of Authority" and a "Christology of Passion" are the two key components of Mark's christological programme. In this regard, C. A. Evans asserts that "Mark's theology consists primarily of Christology..." "Mark," in *New Dictionary of Biblical Theology*, eds. T. Desmond Alexander and Brian S. Rosner (Leicester: IVP, 2000), 269.

[75] "The Authority of Jesus in the Gospel of Mark," *JETS* 37/2 (1994): 217. Edwards succinctly defines Jesus'ἐξουσία as "his sovereign freedom and magisterial authority".

[76] Ibid.

[77] Ibid.

[78] *Studying the New Testament* (London: Epworth Press, 1979), 23.

[79] Hooker shows, for example, that Jesus has and demonstrates authority in proclaiming the Kingdom, in calling disciples, in his astonishing teaching, over unclean spirits/demons, in healings and exorcisms, in forgiving sins, over accepted social conventions, over the Mosaic Law as the "Lord of the Sabbath", through other miracles and parables, in his conflicts with the Jewish religious authorities, over wind and waves and by walking on water ("nature miracles"), in feeding multitudes, and in his ability to restore to life. Ibid., 24-46. Geldenhuys (op. cit.) and D. Martyn Lloyd-Jones also survey Jesus' authority, first in the gospel accounts, then in the other NT documents. See Lloyd-Jones' *Authority* (Edinburgh: BOT, 1992 [1958]), 11-29.

narrative, and represents an or *the* interpretive key for understanding Jesus' person and work.[80] As R. T. France comments, "Jesus appears from the *outset* of Mark's narrative as one who causes astonishment, as *a figure of unprecedented authority*."[81] Lloyd-Jones goes further, suggesting that "the really big claim which is made in the whole of the New Testament, is for the supreme authority of Jesus Christ."[82]

Manifestations of Jesus' ἐξουσία in Mark's Gospel

As will become evident below, the structure and content of Mark's account implies that at least a rough chronological arrangement of events in the life of an influential, historical person is intended. The following summary is based upon a new reading of this gospel that is informed by recognition of authority as the pivotal issue.

1:1-8 In the narrated prologue, the christological title "Son of God"[83] is used for Jesus in v. 1, and in vs. 7-8 the prophet John the Baptist clearly acknowledges Jesus' superior rank or authority. V. 3 quotes Isa. 40:3, and here "Lord" is used in reference to Jesus.

1:9-11 On the occasion of Jesus' baptism by John, a voice from heaven affirms Jesus' sonship, using the christological title "my beloved Son".[84]

---

[80] In the Greek tragedies, *hubris* or some other tragic flaw led to disaster in the lives of protagonists; the story revolved around the hero's struggle with or against that character weakness. In a parallel but opposite fashion, Jesus' authority was the primary characteristic – but not flaw – that led to his influential life and ministry; his authority drove the "plot" of his story. This comparison is not intended to suggest that the gospel genre was in any way modelled after the tragedy, only to note the similar significance of a single prominent characteristic in the flow of a person's life. Admittedly, other readings or interpretive models for Mark have been proposed, e.g., Susan Garrett's model for the tempting or testing of Jesus. See her *The Temptations of Jesus in Mark's Gospel* (Grand Rapids: Eerdmans, 1998). I suggest that these models (authority and testing) are not at loggerheads, but actually are complementary in the scope of God's redemptive purposes.

[81] Emphasis added. *The Gospel of Mark* (NIGTC) (Grand Rapids: Eerdmans, 2002), 25. So Philip Davis, "Mark's Christological Paradox," *JSNT* 35 (1989): 8, writes of the section 1:21-3:6: "Jesus' authority is linked to every major strand of the Gospel story...it is unquestionably central to Mark's Christology."

[82] Op. cit., 15.

[83] Unless noted otherwise, all scripture references herein are from the *English Standard Version*.

[84] James B. Edwards, "The Baptism of Jesus according to the Gospel of Mark," *JETS* 34/1 (1991): 43), notes that "The baptism functions as the cornerstone of Mark's Christological understanding", and suggests that three events at Jesus' baptism – the rending of heaven, the descent of

1:12-13 Jesus is directed by the Spirit into the wilderness, and is targeted by Satan with temptation. This conflict developed into a "showdown" between Jesus and Satan (cf. Mt. 4:1-11).

1:14-15 Jesus expresses authority – by his warrant and freedom – to proclaim the gospel and the kingdom of God.

1:16-20 Jesus calls his first disciples, thus expressing authority as one worthy of leadership and being followed.[85]

1:21-28 In Capernaum, Jesus' teaching in the synagogue is noted for its authority, causing astonishment[86], and his authority is then ratified through his healing a man with an unclean spirit. The unclean spirit recognises Jesus of Nazareth as "the Holy One of God." Ἐξουσία is used in vs. 22 (narrated) and 27 (by crowd).

1:29-34 Jesus expresses his authority by healing many who are ill or oppressed by demons[87], including the mother-in-law of one of his new disciples. [88] He also prevents the demons who recognise him from revealing his identity.

1:35-39 Jesus' authoritative ministries of preaching and exorcism continue throughout Galilee.

---

the Spirit, and the voice of God – indicate not only "the inauguration of God's eschatological kingdom", but also that "Jesus is the inaugurator of that kingdom."

[85] Vernon Robbins, "Mark 1.14-20: An Interpretation at the Intersection of Jewish and Graeco-Roman Traditions," *NTS* 28 (1982): 225, notes that the scene in 1:16-18 'features Jesus commanding the disciples ('come after me'), promising to make them into something they now are not ('I will make you become fishers of men'), and gaining a response from the two men he encounters ('and immediately they left their nets and followed him')." He goes on to liken this to Yahweh's dealing with Abram in Gen. 1:1-4, and glosses (230) "Jesus rather than the Lord God himself decides who will be called into discipleship, and Jesus rather than the Lord God himself issues the commands and promises characteristic of that call." Jesus is "a personage who calls, commands, warns, and promises people with authority delegated to him by Yahweh himself." (233).

[86] Timothy Dwyer, "The Motif of Wonder in the Gospel of Mark," *JSNT* 57 (1995):51, 54, 57, reports that the motif of wonder is used 32 times in Mark, and indicates that "Kingdom authority evidenced in teaching, miracle or pronouncement evokes wonder," remarking that "Wonder is a necessary response to the numinous."

[87] Morna Hooker, *The Gospel according to Saint Mark*, op. cit., 71-75, notes that Mark devotes much space to miracle stories, thus indicating their importance to him. The miracles "not only demonstrate the power of God's Kingdom but reveal the identity of Jesus himself. The authority invested in him is unique – it is the authority of the Son of God." (72). Ernest Best, "The Miracles in Mark," *RevExp* 75/4 (1978): 551, shows that the miracles have a practical significance for disciples in all ages: "The miracles are not merely far-off events in the past life of Jesus but part of the present life of believers."

[88] Grant Osborne, "Structure and Christology in Mark 1:21-45," in *Jesus of Nazareth: Lord and Christ*, eds. Joel B. Green and Max Turner (Grand Rapids: Eerdmans, 1994), 154, suggests that

1:40-45 Jesus wills that a leper be healed, and it is so.[89]

2:1-12 Seeing the faith of the men who bring their paralytic friend to him for healing, Jesus pronounces that the man's sins are forgiven. In response to the questioning hearts of scribes who were witnesses to this "absolution"[90], Jesus proclaims his authority as the "Son of Man" to forgive sins and then proves his authority by healing the paralytic. The crowd is amazed, glorifies God, and says "We never saw anything like this." Ἐξουσία is used in v. 10 (by Jesus, of himself).

2:13-17 Jesus' authority is expressed again in the calling of Levi (Matthew); he says "Follow me" and Levi follows. While dining with sinners, scribes object, and Jesus expresses his mission: to call sinners, not the righteous.

2:18-22 The "otherness" of Jesus as a unique leader is expressed through the non-fasting of his disciples. In Jesus' answer to the people's question, he authoritatively proclaims that he and his message constitute "new wine", symbolising the replacement of scribal Judaism by joyful association with Jesus in God's kingdom.[91]

2:23-28 Pharisees challenge the behaviour of Jesus' disciples and, indirectly, his own authority as their leader. Jesus calls himself the "Son of Man", and "lord even of the Sabbath".

3:1-6 On the Sabbath, Jesus heals a man with a withered hand. In response, the Pharisees and Herodians begin to plot his destruction.

3:7-12 Jesus gains a great following. As unclean spirits recognise Jesus as "the Son of God", he orders them to silence.

Mark's "two sides", christology and discipleship, "blend into a deeper unity" beginning in Mk. 1:29-31 where "Jesus' authority directly touches his disciples' lives".

[89] In healing this leper, offering God's forgiveness (Mk. 2:1-13), ministering on the Sabbath (Mk. 2:23-3:7a), and interpreting food laws (Mk. 7:14-23), Jesus assumes a priestly role. E.g., see the discussion of Broadhead, "Christology as Polemic and Apologetic: The Priestly Portrait of Jesus in the Gospel of Mark," *JSNT* 47 (1992): 29-30, who argues that these "priestly christological images are developed in correspondence with the religious controversy theme", and that this priestly christology is particularly linked to the passion.

[90] Such absolution "is an assurance that is never found in the utterances of any other Jewish prophet. It is unique." James Jones, *The Power and the Glory* (London: Darton, Longman & Todd, 1994): 29.

[91] Brooks, op. cit., 65.

3:13-21 Jesus appoints twelve (whom he also names apostles) "that they might be with him and he might send them out to preach and have authority to cast out demons."[92] Ἐξουσια is used in v. 15 of Jesus' authority delegated to the twelve.

3:22-30 Scribes from Jerusalem attribute Jesus' authority (his warrant and power) to Satan, and Jesus counters with an explanation of blasphemy against the Holy Spirit (the so-called unforgivable sin"), thus claiming divine sanction for his mission.

3:31-35 Jesus proclaims that those who do God's will are his family, thus implicitly claiming a special relationship with God.

4:1-20 In explaining the "Parable of the Sower", Jesus reveals that he knew and understood the "secret of the Kingdom" and would share it with the twelve.

4:21-34 Through his authoritative teaching to the crowd via more parables, Jesus expressed an intimate knowledge of the Kingdom of God; in v. 33, "he spoke the word to them, as they were able to hear (understand) it."

4:35-40 While crossing a lake in a boat, Jesus calms a storm in response to the pleading of his faithless disciples. Their response is one of fear: "Who then is this, that even the wind and sea obey him?" (v. 40).[93]

5:1-20 Jesus heals the Gerasene demoniac. During that encounter, the unclean spirit, through the man, recognised Jesus as "Son of the Most High God" (v. 7). After the man was released from the demon's control, he proclaimed what Jesus had done for him, and everyone marvelled.

---

[92] Jones, op. cit., 59, glosses: "In driving out the demons he is pushing back the frontiers of evil and reclaiming the earth for the rule of God."

[93] Paul Achtemeier, "Person and Deed: Jesus and the Storm-Tossed Sea," *Int* 16/2 (1962): 169-170, contends that there are many stories of individuals who perform miracles, so the fact that Jesus did so does not prove his uniqueness. He argues that "the significance does not lie in the acts themselves but in the person who performs them." The stilling of the storm parallels the Old Testament account of what God does in Ps. 107:28 f. Thus, "Jesus in this pericope is doing what in the Old Testament God alone can do." (174). *Only God* can calm the chaotic and defeat the demonic.

5:21-43 A faith-filled woman, in the midst of a crowd, is healed of a 12-year haemorrhage when she touches Jesus' garment. Subsequently, Jesus went to the home of Jairus, one of the rulers of the synagogue, and raised Jairus' daughter from the dead. Those who come from Jairus' house to report the girl's death call Jesus "the Teacher".

6:1-6 Those who hear Jesus teach in the Nazareth synagogue are astonished by his teaching, and marvel at his wisdom and works. Nevertheless, they took offence at him, and Jesus responded to them with proverbial wisdom concerning the "hometown prophet" lacking honour.

6:7-12 Jesus sends out the twelve two by two, giving them "authority over the unclean spirits." (v. 7). With his delegated authority, "they cast out many demons and anointed with oil many who were sick and healed them." (v. 13). Ἐξουσία is used in v. 7.

6:14-29 The report is given that "Jesus' name had become known", even by King Herod. Seeing the miraculous powers at work in him, Herod and the people generate a variety of explanations.

6:30-44 After teaching a crowd of five thousand men (plus possibly many women and children), he multiplies five fish and two loaves and thus feeds this multitude.

6:45-52 Jesus' authority over nature is demonstrated when he walks on water. The witnesses – his disciples – are astonished.

6:53-56 Having crossed the Sea of Galilee, Jesus' authority is demonstrated as he heals many in the vicinity of Gennesaret.

7:1-13 The Pharisees and scribes from Jerusalem challenge Jesus' authority because his disciples ignore the "tradition of the elders". Jesus, in turn, castigates these Jewish religious leaders because they elevate their traditions above the word of God.[94]

[94] Of such encounters, H. G. G. Herklots comments: "Jesus' whole teaching was set in the context of the Old Testament. Yet those Scriptures were not for Him the casuistical mines surrounded by the slag-heaps of tradition that they were for the Scribes." *Not as the Scribes* (London: SCM, 1934), 26. Jesus did not depart from orthodoxy, only the scribes' warped brand of orthopraxy.

7:14-23 Jesus authoritatively recasts the interpretation of the Law regarding defilement; he declared all foods clean – a shocking pronouncement in opposition to the halakhic tradition.[95]

7:24-30 In recompense for the Syrophoenician woman's faith, Jesus heals her demon-possessed daughter, again displaying his authority over Satan and his minions.

7:31-37 Jesus heals a man of his deafness and a speech impediment in the Decapolis region. The response of the people is again astonishment: "He has done all things well." (v. 37).

8:1-10 Having compassion on a huge crowd, Jesus again multiplies the loaves and miraculously feeds about four thousand people.

8:11-13 The Pharisees come and begin to argue with Jesus, asking for a sign from heaven to test him. They essentially challenge his authority and divine sanction.[96]

8:14-21 Jesus demonstrates his authoritative insight by diagnosing his disciples' faithlessness and lack of understanding.

8:22-26 Jesus again heals, this time a blind man at Bethsaida.

8:27-29 Peter confesses Jesus as "the Christ" (v. 29).

8:31-**9**:1 Jesus again refers to himself as "the Son of Man" and foretells the challenge to and rejection of his authority that would precipitate his death. He also predicts his resurrection and *parousia*, when the Son of Man's authority will be displayed as he comes "in the glory of his Father with the holy angels" (v. 38).

9:2-13 Peter, James and John accompany Jesus up a high mountain where he is transfigured before them. In this passage, Peter refers to Jesus as "Rabbi", a voice from heaven says "this is my

---

[95] Jesus' teaching here "did not abrogate the Mosaic laws on purification or erase the distinction between clean and unclean and declare them invalid. It rather attacked the delusion that sinful men can attain to true purity before God through the scrupulous observance of cultic purity which is powerless to cleanse the defilement of the heart." William L. Lane, *The Gospel according to Mark* (Grand Rapids: Eerdmans, 1974), 254.

[96] Jack Dean Kingsbury, in "The Religious Authorities in the Gospel of Mark," *NTS* 36 (1990): 47, incisively notes that "the issue of authority…underlies every controversy Jesus has with the religious authorities and is, in fact, at the root of his entire conflict with them."

beloved Son; listen to him"[97], and Jesus twice refers to himself as "the Son of Man". Jesus adjures them to silence about this event until after his resurrection, and reminds them that "it is written of the Son of Man that he should suffer many things and be treated with contempt" (v. 12).

9:14-29 A man from the crowd addresses Jesus as "Teacher", and says that he has brought his son for healing; an unclean spirit makes the boy mute, and convulses the boy when it sees Jesus. The faithlessness of the crowd and Jesus' disciples is a blindness to or rejection of Jesus' authority. In response to the father's faith, Jesus casts out the demon, again demonstrating his authority in this realm.

9:30-32 Jesus again demonstrates his authority by correctly foretelling his death and resurrection, and refers to himself as "the Son of Man".

9:33-37 In the course of correcting the selfish aspirations of his disciples, Jesus tells them that "whoever receives me, receives not me but him who sent me." (v. 37). Thus Jesus implicitly claims authority based upon his relationship with God the Father.

9:38-41 John addresses Jesus as "Teacher" as he explains his remonstration of "outsiders" who were exorcising in Jesus' name. Jesus responds: "no one who does a mighty work in my name will be able soon afterwards to speak evil of me."[98] Hereby Jesus claims that there is authority associated with his name and its use, and indirectly refers to himself as "Christ".

9:42-50 In. v. 42, Jesus affirms that he is an object of faith by his statement, "Whoever causes one of these little ones *who believe in me* to sin..." [emphasis added]. He also speaks knowingly concerning entry into the kingdom of God and hell.

---

[97] Francis Glasson, in his "The Uniqueness of Christ: The New Testament Witness," *EvQ* 43/1 (1971): 26-27, refers to Mark 8:27-9:8 and points out that – when Peter mistakenly elevated Jesus to the level of Moses and Elijah – the heavenly voice corrected him by indicating Jesus' uniqueness as the Son, and adjured him/them to "listen to him". Is it pressing the case too much to suggest that this meant to show Jesus as superior to the Law and the Prophets?

[98] Note that Jesus does not say "in God's name". In essence, Jesus here claims authority in the spiritual realm.

10:1-12 As Jesus teaches a crowd, Pharisees come and, "in order to test him", ask Jesus a question about divorce. Their intention clearly is to set Jesus' authority against that of the Mosaic Law.

10:13-16 When the disciples rebuke children for "bothering" Jesus, he remonstrates and instructs them authoritatively concerning who can enter the kingdom of God.

10:17-31 A rich young man approaches Jesus, expecting that Jesus can instruct him regarding conditions for inheriting eternal life. The young man refers to Jesus as "Good Teacher" and "Teacher". Subsequently, Jesus explains not only how the young man could "have treasure in heaven", but also authoritatively and iconoclastically teaches his own disciples about obstacles to entering the kingdom of God and, implicitly, the role of God's grace in salvation. In the course of his teaching, Jesus promises eternal reward to those who have sacrificed *for his sake* and for the gospel.[99]

10:32-34 Jesus, again referring to himself as "the Son of Man", accurately predicts that he will be condemned to death by the religious leaders, then delivered to the Gentiles who will mock, torture and kill him, but will rise from the dead after three days.

10:35-45 Following the inordinate request of James and John for privileged places in the kingdom, Jesus again indicates his knowledge of future events involving himself and these sons of Zebedee. In spite of his authority, Jesus explains, of himself, that "even the Son of Man came not to be served but to serve, and to give his life as a ransom for many" (v. 45), thus again predicting his death.[100] The word "authority", as exercised by the "great ones" of the Gentiles, is used in v. 42, but the Greek word here is the verb form χατεξουσιάζω not the noun ἐξουσία.

---

[99] Trakatellis, op. cit., 66, cogently notes of v. 29: "The important thing is that this sacrifice is made for Jesus. Here Christ becomes the reason for changing relationships and abandoning elementary human goods. This puts emphasis on the divine authority in the person of Jesus."

[100] Peter Lewis, *The Glory of Christ* (Chicago: Moody Press, 1997), 76, suggests that the title "Son of Man" is here linked to the suffering servant of Isa. 53:10.

10:46-52 Jesus again heals, this time the blindness of faith-filled Bartimaeus, who addresses Jesus twice as "Son of David" and once as "Rabbi".

11:1-11 Jesus again predicts future events, this time regarding the disciples' requisitioning of the colt upon which he would ride into Jerusalem. During the "triumphal entry", Jesus is "blessed" by the crowd, who apparently associated his coming with the incipient reestablishment of the kingdom of David.

11:12-14 As an acted parable, Jesus curses a fig tree for its fruitlessness in spite of its appearance of vitality.[101]

11:15-19 Jesus, chagrined and offended by the misuse of the temple, zealously "cleanses" it of merchants, saying "My house shall be called a house of prayer for all the nations". Although quoting Isa. 56:7, he seems to be assuming the authority of God the Father in identifying the temple as his *own* house (cf. Luke 2:49). This action leads to a redoubling of efforts by the chief priests and scribes to destroy Jesus, "for they feared him, because all the crowd was astonished at his teaching." (v. 18).

11:20-25 Seeing that the fig tree that Jesus had cursed has now withered, Peter – calling Jesus "Rabbi" – brings it to Jesus' attention. Jesus uses this to open a lesson on the power of faith-filled prayer. He also refers to the overturning of "this mountain" – a possible hint at the overturning of the temple system.[102]

11:27-33 In the most "in your face" challenge to Jesus' authority in Mark's gospel, chief priests, scribes and elders come to Jesus and ask him "By what authority are you doing these things, or

---

[101] Anne Dawson, op. cit., 182, explains that the fig tree symbolized the *apparent* productivity of the religious establishment which "substituted the true worship of the God of Israel for the trappings of power and greed."

[102] Broadhead provides an interesting explanation of this curious logion ("Which Mountain is 'This Mountain'? A Critical Note on Mark 11:22-25," *Paradigms* 2/1 (1986): 33-38, suggesting that the temple mount symbolically stood "in opposition to genuine faith" and "under the judgement of God"; consequently, the temple would "be replaced by a new fellowship whose faith is centered on God and whose worship is characterized by prayer and forgiveness." (35-36).

who gave you this authority to do them?" (v. 28).[103] Jesus wisely responds with a question regarding the ultimate origin of John's baptism, making his own answer contingent upon their ability to answer his question, and consequently withholds his answer when these religious leaders say "We do not know."[104] Ἐξουσία is used four times in this pericope (vs. 28 [2], 29 and 33).

12:1-12 Through this "Parable of the Tenants", Jesus expounds Israel's historical response to God's offer of redemption as communicated by the prophets, predicts his own death at the hands of God's chosen people, and pronounces God's judgement upon them. The religious leaders well understand that Jesus told the parable against them and, consequently, are seeking to arrest him.

12:13-17 Later some of the Pharisees and Herodians come to Jesus calling him "Teacher", and question him regarding the legality of payment of taxes to Caesar. Jesus' now-famous answer sees through their hypocrisy and plot to trap him. V. 17 reports that their response was one of marvel.

12:18-27 Some Sadducees address Jesus as "Teacher" and ask him a question regarding marriage "in the resurrection". In light of v. 28, which reports that they were "disputing with one another", it seems reasonable to assume that the Sadducees' motives were evil.

[103] Joseph Hellerman has appropriately noted the cultural centrality of honour in the ancient world and, generally, in the Mediterranean region. He suggests that the challenges of the religious leaders were basically challenges to Jesus' claims to honour (here expressed as a claim of divine authority), and that Jesus' responses are culturally programmatic "ripostes", followed by "public verdicts". The crowds' responses to Jesus' answers were always ones of amazement or astonishment, thus enhancing Jesus' honour at the expense of the religious leaders. Thus, the latter lost face and, consequently, status in the society's pecking order. See Hellerman's "Challenging the Authority of Jesus: Mark 11:27-33 and Mediterranean Notions of Honor and Shame," *JETS* 43/2 (2000): 213, 219, 228. Further, Kingsbury, "The Religious Authorities", op. cit., 64, posits that – in Jesus' last great confrontation with the religious authorities (Mk. 11:27-12:34) – "the questions under dispute are all critical in nature and touch, directly or indirectly, on Jesus' authority."

[104] Morna Hooker, *The Gospel according to Saint Mark* (London: A. & C. Black, 1991), 272, comments that "The admission from the religious leaders that they *do not know* is extraordinary: Mark's account of their discussions indicates that he believed them to be deliberately refusing to acknowledge the truth. Jesus' refusal to answer is typical of the way in which he claims authority throughout Mark's gospel. In reality, of course, the answer has been given – but men refuse to accept it as the truth."

Jesus is forthcoming with his answer, accusing them of ignorance both of the Scriptures and also of God's power.

12:28-34 When Jesus is questioned by one of the scribes – who addresses Jesus as "Teacher" – concerning the most important commandment, he judges that this scribe is "not far from the kingdom of God." (v. 34). This perceptive evaluation apparently shocked the crowd, for "after that no one dared to ask him any more questions." (v. 34).

12:35-37 Jesus, teaching in the temple, asks how the Christ could be the son of David when David himself called him Lord, thus demonstrating a remarkable command of the Scriptures and impeccable logic and understanding; "...the great throng heard him gladly." (v. 37). Jesus' analysis of Psalm 110:1 would have been considered a personal claim to messiahship and a clear challenge to the Jewish authorities.[105]

12:38-40 While teaching, Jesus warns his listeners of the false spirituality of the scribes, and renders judgement upon these hypocritical religious leaders.[106]

12:41-44 Jesus demonstrates insight by recognising that the poor widow has put into the offering box all she had to live on.

13:1-2 After one of his disciples remarks about the wonderful buildings in the temple precinct, Jesus accurately predicts the destruction of the temple.

13:3-13 In explaining the signs of the close of the age, Jesus warns his disciples that "Many will come in my name, saying, 'I am he!' and they will lead many astray." (v. 6). This passage is both apocalyptic and eschatological, and implies not only a second coming of Jesus, but also that his followers will suffer persecution and hatred

[105] Ibid., 291-292.

[106] Of this Trakatellis, op. cit., 82, remarks: "His critique against the scribes, exercised with implacable and sweeping language, is a thing which presupposes enormous authority. Only a person endowed with divine prerogative could advance such a public censure of a mighty religious class like the scribes."

for his name's sake. He also declares that those who endure to the end will be saved.

13:14-23 As the authoritative, prophetic teaching of Jesus continues, he warns them of the horrible developments to come, and of false christs and false prophets. He adjures them: "But be on your guard; I have told you all things beforehand." (v. 23).

13:24-27 Jesus predicts that, after these various catastrophic signs of the end, "the Son of Man" (only Jesus uses this title, of himself) will come in the clouds, with great power and glory, and then "he will send out the angels and gather his elect from the four winds, from the ends of the earth to the ends of heaven." (v. 27).

13:28-31 After giving the lesson of the fig tree, Jesus claims astonishing authority and durability for his teaching: "Heaven and earth will pass away, but my words will not pass away." (v. 31).[107]

13:32-37 The long eschatological teaching section draws to a close with Jesus warning them to stay alert, for no one but the Father knows the time that the "master of the house" will come. Jesus emphasises that what he says to them, he says *to all*: "Stay awake." Thus, his warning has global significance.[108]

14:1-2 With the Passover just two days off, the chief priests and scribes – having been startled and threatened by Jesus' authority – seek to secretly arrest and kill him. Fear of the people discourages them from attempting this immediately.

14:3-9 When Jesus is anointed with costly ointment by a woman, some of those present scold her for her profligacy. Conversely, Jesus willingly accepts this act of veneration as a forward-looking preparation for burial, and accurately predicts that her act would be remembered wherever the gospel is proclaimed. This prediction is confirmed by the inclusion of Mark in the NT canon.

---

[107] These words bring to mind Isa. 40:8; on this subject, see R. T. France, *Divine Government*, op. cit., 102.

[108] Accordingly, Sharyn Dowd, *Reading Mark* (Macon: Smith & Helwys, 2000), 137, understands that the "all" in v. 37 indicates all "who may hear [or read] this narrative".

14:10-11 Judas Iscariot, one of Jesus' inner circle, having personally rejected Jesus' authority, betrays Jesus and collaborates with the chief priests in order to bring about Jesus' death.

14:12-21 In instructing two of the disciples to make preparations for the Passover, Jesus accurately predicts some near-future events. He tells them to refer to him as "the Teacher" when enquiring about a venue for their Passover observance. While sharing the meal with the twelve, Jesus correctly foretells his betrayal by one of the twelve, referring to himself twice as "the Son of Man".

14:22-25 Jesus institutes the "Lord's Supper" with the twelve during their Passover observance[109], clearly explaining the substitutionary offering of himself "for many".[110] He also explains that his next drink of "the fruit of the vine" will be in the kingdom.

14:26-31 Again, Jesus accurately foretells near-future events, namely the "falling away" of the twelve and Peter's triad of denials. Peter responds vehemently to this prediction, pledging allegiance even unto death.

14:32-42 Praying in Gethsemane, Jesus familiarly addresses God as "Abba, Father"[111], asking that the Father's will be accomplished in the what lies ahead. Peter, James and John fail to persevere in prayer, and are awakened with these startling words: "...the hour has come. The Son of Man is betrayed into the hands of sinners." (v. 41). Thus Jesus' prediction in 14:18-19 is fulfilled.

---

[109] Dawson, op. cit, 200, posits: "The Passover meal that Jesus has arranged was not intended to be a celebration of Judaism's past. Jesus had repudiated the temple cult, and so *this Passover meal was symbolically articulating another reality*, one that pointed to *a new exodus, a new liberation*." [emphasis added]

[110] Simon J. Gathercole, "The Son of Man in Mark's Gospel," *ExpTim* 115 (2004), 369, aptly notes that "The intention in the Son of Man's advent is not fundamentally the assertion of his authority, but in the accomplishment of the atonement." This perspective explains, to a large degree, the so-called "messianic secret". So Martin Hengel (*Studies in the Gospel of Mark*, London: SCM/XPRESS REPRINTS, 1997 [1985]), 42, adroitly concludes: "Only in suffering does the Marcan Jesus manifest his messianic status in the full sense. Messianic status and representative suffering belong indissolubly together."

[111] Of this expression, I. Howard Marshall, "The Divine Sonship of Jesus," *Int* 21/1 (1967): 90, comments that Jesus "dared to address God by an intimate word that no Jew had ever used, and he initiated his disciples into the same intimate relationship. Jesus thus appears as the mediator of a new relationship with God."

14:43-50 Judas Iscariot addresses Jesus as "Rabbi" and betrays him with a kiss to a crowd who comes from the Jewish religious leaders – who had long questioned and challenged Jesus' authority and plotted his destruction. Jesus yields to this mob, desiring that "the Scriptures be fulfilled" (v. 49). In fulfilment of 14:27, the disciples who were there "all left him and fled." (v. 50).

14:51-52 When seized by Jesus' enemies, one last follower – a young man – fled naked.

14:53-65 In line with their rejection of Jesus' demonstrated authority in many contexts, the chief priests and whole Council arrange a mock trial, complete with false witnesses. When the testimonies of the witnesses disagree, the high priest directly challenges Jesus, asking, "Are you the Christ, the Son of the Blessed?" Jesus' answer is forthright: "I am, and you will see the Son of Man seated at the right hand of Power, and coming with the clouds of heaven." Jesus thus not only reveals his identity fully, but also predicts his future position and glory.[112] The religious leaders deem his response blasphemous, condemn him to death, and abuse him physically and verbally.

14:66-72 Peter fulfils Jesus' prediction by denying him thrice. Jesus is referred to as "the Nazarene" by a servant girl of the high priest.

15:1-5 The Council sent Jesus to Pilate, the Roman governor, who asks: "Are you the King of the Jews?" (v. 2)[113]. Jesus' response, "You have said so", is neither direct affirmation nor explicit denial. Pilate is amazed by Jesus' silence to charges made against him.

---

[112] Christopher Bryan, in his *A Preface to Mark* (New York/Oxford: OUP, 1993): 117-118, comments astutely on Jesus' answer: "As in his first public responses to his critics he claimed for himself the authority of the Son of man in forgiveness and in lordship over the Sabbath (2:10, 28), so now in his last public words he claims the authority of the Son of man in judgment. Such a claim might seem like madness: yet when, a few minutes later, we return to the courtyard and to the fulfilment of his prophecy regarding Peter's denial, this merely confirms our impression that he is the one who is in charge here, despite all appearances to the contrary."

[113] Edwards (*The Gospel according to Mark*, op. cit., 458) writes: "As in the case of the high priest, Mark's wording makes Pilate an unknowing confessor. Again, even the mouths of Jesus' enemies unwittingly confess him."

15:6-15 In this pericope, Pilate – while speaking to a crowd – twice more calls Jesus "King of the Jews". V. 10 reports that Pilate perceived that the impetus for the chief priests' action of delivering Jesus up to him was their envy, thus confirming that they believed their authority was threatened by his. The crowd presses for insurrectionist Barabbas' release, precipitating first the scourging of Jesus then his being taken for crucifixion.

15:16-20 Roman soldiers mockingly pay homage to Jesus, giving him a crown and purple robe, kneeling before him and hailing him as "King of the Jews".

15:21-32 At the scene of his crucifixion, Jesus' garments are divided among the soldiers who cast lots for them, thus apparently fulfilling Ps. 22:18. The inscription of the charges against Jesus identifies him as the "King of the Jews", and Jewish religious leaders mock him saying "He saved others, he cannot save himself. Let the Christ, the King of Israel, come down now from the cross that we may see and believe." (v. 31-32). Two aspects of this statement are noteworthy: their admission that Jesus saved others, and the recognition that Jesus' claim to authority was such that it commanded belief that he is a saviour. That is, Jesus was understood to be an object of faith.

15:33-41 At Jesus' death, the temple curtain is torn in two[114], and the attending centurion says "Truly this man was the Son of God."[115]

15:42-47 Joseph of Arimathea, "a respected member of the Council who was also himself looking for the kingdom of God" (v. 43), courageously asks Pilate for the body of Jesus. He has Jesus' body

[114] Both Howard Jackson ("The Death of Jesus in Mark and the Miracle from the Cross," *NTS* 33 (1987): 16-37) and David Ulansey ("The Heavenly Veil Torn: Mark's Cosmic 'Inclusio'," *JBL* 110/1 (1991): 123-125) suggest that it was the outer veil of the temple that was torn at Jesus' death. Furthermore, Ulansey's argument – that the motif of tearing in Mark (at the *precise beginning* [the rending of the heavens at his baptism] and *precise ending* [the rending of the veil at his death] of Jesus' earthly ministry) is the powerful and intentional use of a symbolic "inclusio" – is compelling.

placed in a newly hewn tomb, apparently thus fulfilling the words of Isa. 53:9: "with a rich man in his death."

16:1-8 An angel reports the resurrection of "Jesus of Nazareth, who was crucified" to women who have come to the tomb to anoint him. The women are shown the empty tomb, and told to report what they have seen and heard to the disciples, and that Jesus is going before them to Galilee. The women's response was "trembling and astonishment". Jesus' authority over death – even his own – is proven (cf. 6:35-43, 15:31).

16:9-20 Most scholars consider this section to be a later addition. Nevertheless, as James Edwards notes, it is likely that Mark's original manuscript did not, in fact, end at v. 8. He explains that Matthew's account closely follows that of Mark, at least in the subject matter dealt with. In so far as the critically important "Great Commission", with Jesus' claim to possess "all authority in heaven and on earth" (Mt. 28:18), is absent in the earliest extant manuscripts of Mark's gospel, Edwards suggests that the autograph of Mark's account probably *did* include accounts of Jesus' post-resurrection appearances and a statement of the Great Commission.[116]

It is clear from this survey of Mark's account that its subject, beginning to end, is Jesus. The purpose of the foregoing annotations is to show that Jesus *claims*, *implies* or *demonstrates* his authority to forgive sins, over demonic forces, illness and death, and nature; and in his relationships to God, the disciples, the crowd, and his adversaries. In places, others – demons, followers, strangers, and opponents – *recognise*, *affirm*, *challenge* or *reject* Jesus' authority. In line with the reading of Mark's gospel above, James Edwards offers this provocative analysis at the close of his survey of Jesus' authority as presented in Mark's account:

---

[115] Tae Hun Kim, "The Anarthrous υἱός θεοῦ in Mark 15.39 and the Roman Imperial Cult, " *Bib* 79 (1998): 241, contends that "to the author of the Gospel of Mark there was no doubt that the centurion confirmed the divine sonship of Jesus marking the climax of the narrative."

[116] *The Gospel according to Mark*, op. cit., 501-504.

> Thus in the gospel of Mark, as in John, Jesus appears as God incarnate in his bearing, speech and activity. This astonishes, baffles, and even offends his contemporaries, from his closest circles outward. The religious leaders in particular regard his laying claim to a realm that belonged to God as the gravest possible trespass. Jesus gives the distinct impression, however, that he is not a trespasser but is entering into his rightful property.[117]

There is hardly a pericope in Mark's gospel that does not, either explicitly or implicitly, turn on the issue of Jesus' authority. It is concluded that the ultimate rejection of Jesus' authority was what precipitated the other major christological emphasis of Mark's account, namely, Jesus' passion. From a simply human perspective, had Jesus not claimed or demonstrated authority, his passion would not have been necessitated. In God's economy, however, Jesus' passion was not only necessary, but also the climax of God's plan of redemption.

---

[117] "The Authority of Jesus", op. cit., 233.

4. THE QUESTIONS OF INTENT AND GENRE

We have seen that authority is a major theme in, if not an (or *the*) interpretive key to understanding, Mark's account of Jesus' life and ministry.[118] However, the significance of this observation might be open to question unless we first understand the intent of the biblical author. What did Mark[119] hope to accomplish with this composition? What did he want the readers/listeners of his account "to come away with"? [120] Was there an error that he hoped to correct[121], or a particular response that he hoped to engender, in the audience he addressed?

As we approach any piece of literature, the question of genre is of great importance. Understanding of genre[122] drives the reader's or

---

[118] Frank Matera, "The Prologue as the Interpretive Key to Mark's Gospel, " in *The Interpretation of Mark* (2nd ed.), ed. William Telford (Edinburgh: T. & T. Clark, 1995), 302, proposes that the information found in Mk. 1:2-13, the book's prologue, is the "hermeneutical key" to this gospel, and stresses that this information "must be read by the light of the cross." This conclusion really does not differ from my own in so far as the information to which Matera refers is mainly christological and, specifically, is replete with allusions to Jesus' authority. Allen Mawhinney, "Baptism, Servanthood, and Sonship," *WTJ* 49 (1987), 42, also argues that the Markan prologue constitutes "the key for understanding the entire gospel." On another note, the caveats of Earl Johnson ("Is Mark 15.39 the Key to Mark's Christology?," *JSNT* 31 (1987): 15), and R. T. France ("Mark and the Teaching of Jesus," in *Gospel Perspectives*, eds. R. T. France and David Wenham (Sheffield: JSOT Press, 1980), 101), are well taken. Johnson warns that it is dangerous to assume that a single theme is a necessary key to an entire Gospel, and France contends: "It is...unrealistic to elevate a particular slant which may be discovered at certain points in the gospel into the determining principle by which all the contents of the book are judged." Nevertheless, the ubiquity of pericopae that directly or indirectly touch on the issue of Jesus' authority is compelling and, thus, certainly worthy of our attention.

[119] Because scholars debate the authorship, the *Sitz im Leben* of the evangelist and his audience, and the exact date of the composition of Mark (generally accepted to be between 55-75 A.D.), it is imprudent to be dogmatic about these issues. For the sake of simplicity, I will use the traditional attribution throughout.

[120] These questions are not intended to imply a denial of the divine purpose and inspiration of this account (e.g. 2 Tim 3:16). Ultimately, as Robertson McQuilkin notes, "Any teaching derives its authority from that inherent in its source." (*Understanding and Applying the Bible* [revised edition], Chicago: Moody Press, 1992 [1983], 275). Thus, the biblical text is authoritative because its ultimate source is God. The issue in the present context is *authorial intent* as a basis for interpretation. For a clear statement of the present writer's position on inspiration and the authority of Scripture, see Appendix 1.

[121] E.g., T. J. Weeden, "The Heresy that Necessitated Mark's Gospel," *ZNW* 59 (1968): 145-158, suggests that Mark wrote to correct a false christology, namely that of the θείος άνήρ ("divine man").

[122] Ched Myers and his co-authors, *'Say to this Mountain': Mark's Story of Discipleship* (Maryknoll, New York, 1996), 214-215, prefer the term "architecture" to genre, and compares it – in the analogy of a building – to the master floor plan.

listener's expectations from and interpretation of the text.[123] As Adela Collins has noted,

> The decision about the genre of Mark is not merely a matter of taxonomy or academic scholarship. One's assumptions about the literary form of Mark affect the way this work is allowed to function in the lives of readers, in the life of the church, and in society.[124]

Robertson McQuilkin's guidelines related to authorial intent and, more generally, to understanding human language, are helpful, and are adopted herein by the present writer: "Seek the ordinary meaning of the language. Identify the literary style of the language. Seek the single meaning intended by the author."[125] In most situations, unless an author – biblical or otherwise – makes it clear, we typically do *and* should operate on the assumption that there is a single, definite meaning for a document produced by said author.[126] Accordingly, as we approach Mark's gospel, we assume that he had a particular design for his account.

Scholars differ in their opinions about the genre of Mark's account. Was he writing a history; a biography; an evangelistic or hortatory sermon; a story, novel or "narrative"; or was the "gospel" a new genre first produced by Mark?

Before surveying these various proposals, a preliminary comment is in order. As Martin notes, it seems that Mark was the originator of the term "gospel" (εὐαγγέλιον) in so far as there is no

---

[123] A simple example is "Take my wife…please!" If these words are spoken by a stand-up comedian, we would understand one thing, but if spoken by a concerned husband to a rescue crew after a mountaineering accident, quite another.

[124] *The Beginning of the Gospel: Probings of Mark in Context* (Eugene, Oregon: Wipf and Stock, 2001 [Augsburg Fortress, 1992]), 2. So Telford, *The Theology of the Gospel of Mark* (Cambridge: CUP, 1999), 6, who writes: "Establishing the genre of a literary work provides us with our first clue as to its origin, meaning and purpose, and *without such indications, the theology cannot be fully appreciated.*" [emphasis added].

[125] Op. cit., 85-89.

[126] Contra Susan Garrett, op. cit., 9, who – although she acknowledges that knowledge of the Mark's intent might help readers/hearers interpret a text – suggests that such knowledge does not exhaust the meaning of Mark's text, and stresses that "the meaning of the text overflows the bounds of 'authorial intent'." While I would agree that human finitude is an obstacle or limitation in our

evidence for its use in any of the pre-Markan traditions.[127] The non-Christian usage of the term was in reference to good news, such as of a victory in battle or the enthronement of a ruler.[128]

The word seems to be a favourite of the evangelist; he uses εὐαγγέλιον seven times, while John never uses "gospel", and Luke never uses it as a noun.[129] Hengel points out that, at the beginning of the Markan account, εὐαγγέλιον Ἰησοῦ Χριστοῦ is used as an objective genitive meaning "the gospel *about* Jesus Christ i.e. the saving events of the ministry and death of Jesus in the 'biographical' work that is now beginning."[130] Thus, as far as Mark is concerned, the content of this gospel account is the whole εὐαγγέλιον Ἰησοῦ Χριστοῦ, and this is the introduction of the book.[131] On the other hand, Telford suggests that Mark used the term to "describe Jesus' teaching without, however, specifying its precise content." Telford *does* admit that the content of the message may be either by *or* about Jesus.[132] In that Mark's gospel contains less of Jesus' teaching than any of the other gospel accounts, it seems wise to favour Hengel's position. Therefore, we can expect the balance of the Markan account to focus on Jesus' life and work in general, not just or especially on the content of his teaching.

Regardless of to which genre it is assigned, Mark's account concentrates on Jesus. William Lane suggests that, although this gospel is "neither a formal historical treatise nor a biography of Jesus", it still must be considered an historical narrative *and*

---

hermeneutic endeavour, to tie the meanings of ancient texts (especially ones with claims to divine provenance) to the impressions or responses of the reader is dangerously subjective.

[127] Op. cit., 24. Contra Martin Hengel, op. cit., 54, who suggests that this terminology (i.e., gospel) "was certainly not the personal invention of Mark" but, rather, was dependent on earlier terminology.

[128] Martin, ibid., 22.

[129] Hengel, op.cit. 53.

[130] Ibid. Contra Eugene Lemcio who posits: "Jesus is not the content of the εὐαγγέλιον in the narrative". "The Intention of the Evangelist, Mark," *NTS* 32 (1986): 190.

[131] Ibid., 158, n. 81.

[132] Op. cit., 4-5.

proclamation – a "witness document".[133] Thus, Mark's gospel is a kind of kerygmatic history. Collins also examines the general proposals that Mark wrote a "gospel", a biography or spiritual biography (aretalogy), or history. Her view is that, in spite of the fact that Mark indeed "focuses on Jesus and his identity", his intention was to write a particular kind of history, namely an *historical monograph.*[134] Likewise, Nineham accepts Mark's account as a "connected historical narrative", and rejects its designation as biography *sensu stricto.*[135] Siegfried Schulz, too, suggests that to Mark "gospel" meant history.[136]

Hengel calls the four gospel accounts "kerygmatic biographies", and tentatively ties Mark's usage of εὐαγγέλιον to the Petrine understanding of the gospel.[137] While not necessarily rejecting the historicity of the Markan narrative, Achtemeier prefers to recognise the account simply as *proclamation.*[138] He recognises Mark's gospel as "something new within the Christian community", noting that "For the first time that we can determine, the Jesus traditions were understood as a 'story' in the Gospel of Mark".[139]

Elizabeth Malbon calls Mark's account "story", but stresses that "To recognize that Mark's Gospel was written as a story does not answer the question of its historical accuracy…".[140] Edwin Broadhead, also makes the "story" assignment, at the same time

---

[133] Op. cit., 1. Similarly Schweizer, *The Good News according to Mark* (London: SPCK, 1971), 24, notes that Mark's account lacks the essential characteristics of a biography, and more resembles "a volume of sermons" than the former. However, even though he affirms the kerygmatic content of the book, he sees it as, fundamentally, "a history book".

[134] Op. cit., 27, 37. Collins clarifies: "The Gospel of Mark combines realistic historical narrative with an eschatological perspective." (34). She admits that Mark is not history in the same way as Thucydides, but instead in an "eschatological or apocalyptic sense." (37).

[135] D. E. Nineham, *Saint Mark* (Harmondsworth: Penguin, 1963), 35-36. He points out that Mark's gospel neither has the earmarks of a biography nor fulfils the goals of such. See also Joel F. Williams, "Discipleship and Minor Characters in Mark's Gospel," *BSac* 153 (1996): 333, who calls Mark's account "a narrative, that is, a narration of a series of events. The Gospel of Mark is a historical narrative, but it is a narrative nonetheless."

[136] "Mark's Significance for the Theology of Early Christianity," in *The Interpretation of Mark*, ed. William Telford (London: SPCK, 1985), 158-159.

[137] Op. cit., 54, 58.

[138] Op. cit., 21.

[139] Ibid., 6.

[140] *Hearing Mark* (Harrisburg, Pennsylvania: Trinity Press, 2002), 4.

claiming that the form and content of Mark's account suggest a "kerygmatic function".[141] In his estimation, Mark is all about proclamation, with Jesus as the message being trumpeted. Elsewhere, in fact, Broadhead refers to scenes in Mark 14-16 as *pronouncement reports within a passion context.*[142] Of these scenes he writes:

> These stories employ a pattern found throughout the Gospel of Mark: the words of Jesus are incorporated into his story in such a way that they recall his mission and re-present his message as a living voice for his followers.[143]

Yet another viewpoint on the subject of genre is that of Vernon Robbins, who both argues for the distinctiveness of Mark, but also notes that parallels and influences from both Jewish and Greco-Roman cultural streams shape this work, which is biographic in form.[144] Likewise, Christopher Bryan argues in detail that Mark's gospel shares many characteristics with what he designates a Hellenistic "life"; it is a biographical prose narrative wherein Jesus is always the "true center of concern".[145]

Tolbert, Lemcio and Vorster all view Mark's account as a synthetic literary narrative. Tolbert likens Mark's gospel to *ancient popular novels*, and sees conspicuous "rhetorical, stylistic, and linguistic similarities" between them.[146] Lemcio urges that Mark's narrative should be examined as "an integrated whole" from the perspective of literary analysis, and emphasises that Mark "narrates christology-in-the-making".[147] Drawing on the methods and conclusions of literary-critical studies of the gospels, Vorster claims

---

[141] *Mark* (Sheffield: SAP, 2001), 146. See also Broadhead's *Prophet, Son, Messiah: Narrative Form and Function in Mark 14-16* (Sheffield: JSOT Press, 1994), esp. 25-26, 292-296.

[142] "Form and Function in the Passion Story: The Issue of Genre Reconsidered," *JSNT* 61 (1996): 26.

[143] Ibid.

[144] *Jesus the Teacher* (Philadelphia: Fortress, 1984), 4, 5, 10.

[145] Op. cit., 23-25, 39, 62-63. So Achtemeier, *Mark* (op. cit., 53), who claims that "there is no question that for the Gospel of Mark, Jesus is the central figure. If he is not present in every scene, he is the subject around which every narrative turns, and it is his activity and fate that are Mark's chief concern."

[146] *Sowing the Gospel* (Minneapolis: Fortress, 1989), 78.

[147] Op. cit., 188, 200.

that “the narrative character of the gospel genre calls into question both kerygma and history as distinctive characteristics of the gospel genre.”[148] Conversely, Robert Tannehill, who also views Mark’s gospel as a narrative composition, stresses that his approach “is not opposed to historical research.”[149]

Howard Kee surveys a number of possibilities in order to determine if Mark had a literary paradigm for his gospel.[150] His conclusion is that, although Mark apparently was influenced by Hellenistic culture, and shares some characteristics with the eschatological-apocalyptic literature of post-exilic Judaism, the “gospel” is a wholly new genre created by Mark.[151] Similarly, Martin both recognises the newness of the gospel genre, and also notes that the gospel accounts “are kerygmatic in nature and evangelical in design.”[152] As such, a particular response is expected or desired from the reading or listening audience.

While this range of opinions may seem daunting at first glance, I suggest that the “problem” is not as serious as it may seem. With relatively few exceptions, most serious Markan scholars do not see Mark’s account as fictive or fabricated.[153] Rather, there is a widespread willingness to accept the proposal that Mark believed and

---

[148] “Kerygma/History and the Gospel Genre,” *NTS* 29 (1983): 91.

[149] “The Gospel of Mark as Narrative Christology,” *Semeia* 16/1 (1979): 60.

[150] He evaluated these possibilities: aretalogy; Greek tragedy; “origin myth”; Hellenistic romance; comedy; martyrology; Hellenistic *chria*; and miracle story. *Community of the New Age: Studies in Mark’s Gospel* (London: SCM, 1977), 17-30.

[151] Ibid., 30. So James Brooks, who rejects proposals that Mark’s gospel is history or biography in the modern sense. He notes that this account has much in common with many genres, but “does not correspond exactly to any of them.” Op. cit., 25.

[152] Martin, op. cit., 21.

[153] Even most scholars who approach Mark’s account using the methods of narrative and redaction criticism do not suggest that Mark either was or intended to be fanciful or duplicitous. In fact, William Lane (op. cit., 7) stresses: “There is no necessary reason why redaction criticism should lead to the de-historicising of the NT Gospel.” Elizabeth Malbon (op. cit., 3), who prefers to call Mark’s gospel “story”, suggests that “*The Gospel was written by someone who believes that Jesus is the Christ, the Son of God*, assumes that the audience believes that too, and wants to show the audience how their life together can be deeper and richer – and how their community can move out into the broader world because of that.” [emphasis added]. Conversely, by assigning Mark’s account to the category of simple literary narrative, Tolbert, Lemcio and Vorster (op. cit.) effectively reject the traditional evangelical understanding of inspiration and also the veracity of any aspects of Mark’ gospel that might be traditionally considered historical. This is not to say that these authors themselves have no faith commitments, nor that they find no kerygmatic value in Mark’s account.

intended to present an account that was factual[154], not propagandistic. In other words, Mark's gospel should be accepted as *a work of non-fiction* that aimed to accurately *and* persuasively present the person and work of Jesus. Lane's perspective on this account is helpful:

> The assertion that Mark made historical events subservient to his theological purpose demands the affirmation that there were *historical events.* The theological import of these events is dependent upon the activity of God in Jesus of Nazareth. While the theological significance of the historical facts must not be denied, it must also be maintained that their theological meaning is dependent upon their historical occurrence. Ultimately it is the creative life of Jesus Christ, not the evangelists or their communities, that originates, controls and gives essential unity to the documents through which witness is borne to his achievement as the Messiah, the Son of God (Mark 1:1).[155]

Furthermore, although his account certainly possesses aspects common to the biographical[156] and historical genres, it is also clearly kerygmatic or rhetorical[157]. This combination of characteristics may point toward recognition of a new "gospel" genre[158], but to try and force Mark's gospel into a single category is neither necessary nor wise. Broadhead, in an analysis of Mark 14:1-9, suggests that

> For Mark, "gospel" is the story of the coming of God's good news in the journey of Jesus. It is the story of a messiah whose definitive sign is the cross. It is the story of God' [sic] redeeming fellowship with sinners. It is a story which demands a response

---

[154] Reflecting the actual situation or truth. As A. T. Robertson (op. cit., 75) writes, "The stamp of reality is in this story." E.g., Ernest Best, in his *Following Jesus* (Sheffield: JSOT Press, 1981), 11, suggests that "there is no reason to doubt that he [Mark] believed what he wrote had in broad outline actually happened."

[155] "From Historian to Theologian: Milestones in Markan Scholarship," *RevExp* 75/4 (1978): 613-614.

[156] We would do well to keep in mind that, after all, biography *is* a subset or type of history.

[157] E.g., see George A. Kennedy, *New Testament Interpretation through Rhetorical Criticism* (Chapel Hill, NC: UNC Press, 1984), 97-113.

[158] Telford notes the most prudent position: "...since there is no such thing as a literary genre which has no roots in antecedent literary types, the most we can say is that Mark's Gospel represents a new type of 'evolved' literature for which numerous 'partial antecedents' in the ancient world can be suggested." Introduction to *The Interpretation of Mark*, ed. William Telford (London: SPCK, 1985), 9. In the same vein, Morna Hooker, op. cit., 11-12, writes that "nothing is ever entirely new", so "attempts to discover partial antecedents in various literary models have continued."

> from its hearer/reader. If taken seriously, this self-definition has wide implications for the understanding of the character and purpose of Mark's gospel and for the further understanding of the genre of gospel.[159]

Although academic thoroughness demands that the issue of genre receive our attention, this is one pursuit which may ultimately be fruitless for Mark's account; the multitude of dissonant voices will not likely be harmonised. My intent here has not been to erect a "straw man" and then promptly tear it down; rather, I desire to give due consideration to a significant issue and, from it, to springboard to the one of the core issues in dealing with Mark's account.

What really matters is that Mark's gospel and its subject, Jesus, are evaluated in the way intended by its author. Achtemeier claims that Mark uses the term "gospel" in a special way – it is more than a book, or a narrative or a collection of facts; Jesus' power operates through it, and it "is able to save a person's life."[160]

Therefore, as readers or listeners interact with this account, the challenge is to *understand* and *respond* to the Jesus that Mark knew of and proclaimed, the one with authority *sans pareil*. He is the one who is able to change and save lives.

---

[159] "Mark 14:1-9: A Gospel within a Gospel," *Paradigms* 1/1 (1985): 40.
[160] *Mark*, op. cit., 64.

5. TITULAR CHRISTOLOGY: A FERTILE OR AN ARID FIELD?

In Mark's, and the other gospels, Jesus' words and works were a source of astonishment or amazement for his supporters and opponents alike. He foretold near- and distant-future events and, to date, all have come to pass – thus confirming his prophetic office. But the authority he claimed exceeded that of a prophet, and his teaching and miraculous actions in a wide variety of situations were manifestations of his divine authority.

One way that Mark attempts to communicate the significance of Jesus' person and work – apart from the narrative he provides – is through the use of special titles, the most studied being *Son of Man* and *Son of God*. However, Mark[161] also uses other titles, such as *the Nazarene/Jesus of Nazareth, beloved Son, the Holy One of God, the Christ, the Son of the Blessed, Son of the Most High God, Teacher, Rabbi, a prophet, Son of David*, and *the King of the Jews/the King of Israel*, as noted in Chapter 3. For an explanation of the Old Testament roots of the key titles, the monograph of Joel Marcus is recommended.[162]

In places, the titles are recorded in narrated sections. Elsewhere they come from Jesus' own lips, are used by his disciples, or are uttered by ostensible allies or ones who have been positively influenced by Jesus' ministry. Jesus' opponents – such as the Jewish religious leaders – or other antagonists generate some of the titles, using them either in flattering, mocking or accusing fashion.

Christians historically have understood these titles not simply as honorific, but also have assumed that some reflect Jesus' divinity. Conversely, many scholars – lacking the same theological/

---

[161] Or those involved in the narrative/his characters.
[162] *The Way of the Lord* (Edinburgh: T. & T. Clark, 1993).

confessional commitments – have seemingly attempted to empty these titles of significance or any real meaning. The question before us concerns the import of these titles in light of the above reading of Mark's account, and specifically as applied to the case of Turkish culture.

Christological Tunnel Vision

Leander Keck laments that scholars have "often assumed that New Testament christology *is* a matter of the history of titles", and posits that

> no other factor has contributed more to the aridity of the discipline than this fascination with the palaeontology of christological titles. To reconstruct the history of titles as if this were the study of Christology is like trying to understand the windows of the Chartres cathedral by studying the history of coloured glass.[163]

This plaintive cry has been echoed by Larry Chouinard:

> One must avoid the assumption that an examination of titles within the narrative exhaust the Christology of a Gospel. The preoccupation with titles has often caused a failure to grasp the rich detail of a Gospel's christological presentation.[164]

R. T. France also joins the chorus, emphasising that Mark's narrative and theological statements cannot be boiled down to a few titles; Mark's point is that the whole gospel is christology.[165] The story interprets the titles, not *vice versa*. With this caveat in mind, the possible significance of some of Mark's christological titles is briefly surveyed below.

Son of God

When used in Mark's narrative, how did hearers respond to this title? Joel Marcus discusses in detail the question posed to Jesus in Mk. 14:61 – "Are you the Christ (Messiah), the Son of the Blessed

---

[163] "Toward the Renewal of New Testament Christology," *NTS* 32 (1986): 368.
[164] "Gospel Christology: A Study of Methodology," *JSNT* 30 (1987): 28.

(God)?" – and his response. Marcus suggests that Jesus' answer "would have fallen on Jewish ears as a claim to commensurability with God."[166] Even without Marcus' careful analysis of the pre-New Testament background of this bipartite title, it seems obvious from the context that the attendant Jewish leaders were horrified by what they considered a blasphemous claim.

Of this title, James Edwards argues convincingly against an adoptionistic understanding of Jesus' baptism in Mk. 1:9-11, noting that Jesus' "status of Sonship...precedes the function of Messiahship." Confirmation of his Sonship at his baptism inaugurated his ministry of servanthood.[167] His sonship was further confirmed at the transfiguration – where Jesus was singled out as God's beloved Son – indicating clearly his superiority to Moses and Elijah[168], and that "his origin belongs to the heavenly world."[169] France calls this title "the real truth about Jesus", and Kingsbury's monograph on Mark's christology eloquently argues that "Son of God" is Mark's central christological category.[170]

Hengel and Collins argue convincingly against recasting this title to mean simply a Hellenistic "divine man". Although this was once a popular explanation for vanquishing the claims of the Markan Jesus, Hengel submits

> that Jesus' miracles are a reference to the messianic exousia of Jesus and an expression of the eschatological fulfilment of prophetic promise. Both these things cannot be understood in terms of the worn-out catchphrase theios anēr.[171]

---

[165] *The Gospel of Mark*, op. cit., 24. See also Boring, "Markan Christology: God-Language for Jesus?," *NTS* 45 (1999): 461.

[166] "Mark 14:61: 'Are You the Messiah-Son-of-God?" *NovT* 31/2 (1989): 141. So Davis, "Mark's Christological Paradox," op. cit., 10-11.

[167] "The Baptism of Jesus," op. cit., 57.

[168] Morna Hooker, "Mark," in *It is Written,* eds. D. A. Carson & H. G. M. Williamson (Cambridge: CUP, 1988), 226-227.

[169] Dieter Zeller, "New Testament Christology in its Hellenistic Reception," *NTS* 46 (2001): 326.

[170] E.g., France, *Divine Government*, op. cit., 103; Kingsbury, *The Christology of Mark's Gospel* (Philadelphia: Fortress, 1983), e.g., 142, 173-174.

[171] Op. cit., 41. For a similar conclusion, see also Kingsbury, "The 'Divine Man' as the Key to Mark's Christology – The End of an Era?" *Int* 35/3 (1981): 246-257, esp. 248-252; and Broadhead, *Teaching with Authority* (Sheffied: JSOT Press, 1992), 210-213.

Collins reports that there was, in the past, a broad consensus among Mark scholars concerning the "divine man" interpretation, but notes that "that virtual consensus has not stood the test of time."[172]

Son of Man

Achtemeier comments that the titles "Christ" and "Son of God" do not figure as prominently in the narrative as does "Son of Man"[173], noting that only Jesus uses this title – the one that best reflects Mark's christology.[174] Further, he suggests that this title describes Jesus' destiny more than his identity in so far as it is mainly used in reference to the passion.[175]

Guelich submits that this title possesses little christological weight, concluding that it "denoted a self-designation by Jesus but carried little of the christological or messianic overtones of 'Messiah' and 'Son of God' for Mark."[176] Similarly, Harrison suggests that the title *is* "non-committal", yet highly significant in the way Jesus used it: it served as "a mere skeleton which became a living entity when used to express His glory consequent upon humiliation as an ideal and representative human being."[177] He considers the title, as employed by Jesus, to hint both at supremacy and power, and elsewhere at weakness, humiliation and suffering.[178]

Eugene Boring argues that the meaning of "Son of Man" specifies the contents of "Christ" and "Son of God", noting that the principal meaning of the former for Mark "is that he is the suffering, dying, and rising one who will return in glory."[179]

---

[172] Op. cit., 60.

[173] *Mark*, op. cit., 53.

[174] Ibid., 58.

[175] Ibid., 59.

[176] Op. cit., 521. So Barnabas Lindars, *Jesus, Son of Man* (Grand Rapids: Eerdmans, 1984), 106, who claims that this title has no particular christological content in itself, but gains such from the context; and Seyoon Kim, *The Son of Man as the Son of God* (Grand Rapids: Eerdmans, 1985 [1983]), who basically equates the two titles.

[177] "The Son of Man," *EvQ* 23/1 (1951): 50.

[178] Ibid., 46.

[179] "The Christology of Mark: Hermeneutical Issues for Systematic Theology," *Semeia* 30 (1985): 132.

A striking feature of Mark's usage of this title "is its intimate association with the motif of Jesus' authority."[180] Likewise, Gathercole recognizes the following narrative pattern that holds the Son of Man sayings together: *"the authoritative Son of Man revealed – the authority of the Son of Man rejected – the authority of the Son of Man vindicated"*[181] – and this "Son of Man" proves himself to be a man who does what only God can do.[182] Thus, although "Son of Man" may literally mean simply "the man" or "the human being", it "applies to Jesus in a way in which it can be applied to no other human being."[183] France writes:

> If the "Son of Man" in Mark's Gospel is understood against its Old Testament background, it takes its place as part of Mark's presentation of Jesus as more than human.[184]

Jesus of Nazareth/ the Nazarene

Broadhead surveys the use of Nazarene imagery in Mark's gospel. In his study, he chose the "inherently empty and ambiguous" term in order to bring into focus the role of christological titles in Mark's gospel.[185] He notes in particular its "strategic placement at key junctures of Jesus' story", and that it is "ultimately joined to the image of Jesus the Crucified One." [186]

Finally, Eugene Boring reaches the interesting conclusion that "Mark uses no specific God-Language of Jesus", yet hastens to add that Mark has a high christology and affirms the deity of Christ.

---

[180] Philip Davis, "Mark's Christological Paradox," op. cit., 9. So Boring, ibid., 133; Lindars, op. cit., 102-103; Bryan, op. cit., 145; D. J. Doughty, "The Authority of the Son of Man (Mk.2:1-3:6)," *ZNW* 74 (1983): 168; and Hooker, *The Son of Man in Mark* (London: SPCK, 1967), 179, who writes: "...the vital point with which they [the Son of Man sayings] are *all* linked is the question of Jesus' authority – the authority which he claims and which his followers accept."

[181] Op. cit., 371-372.

[182] Ibid.

[183] Kingsbury, *Conflict in Mark* (Minneapolis: Fortress, 1989), 58-60.

[184] *Divine Government*, op. cit., 103.

[185] "Jesus the Nazarene: Narrative Strategy and Christological Imagery in the Gospel of Mark," *JSNT* 52 (1993): 17.

[186] Ibid., 17-18. On the issue of its placement, it occurs in 1:9 in the initial portrait of Jesus, in 1:21-38 on the first day of Jesus' ministry, in 10:46-52 in a healing scene displaying his power, in 14:67 in the conflict/abandonment situation of his trial, and in 16:1-8 at his resurrection.

Boring glosses: "For Mark, to tell the story of *Jesus* is to talk about *God*, the *one* God."[187]

We must deal with the titles because they figure prominently in Mark's narrative. But what if they did not? Would our estimation of Jesus – his person, teaching and works – change drastically? While the titles *do* clarify or confirm key aspects of Jesus' identity, they collectively are not, as shown above, the *sine qua non* of Mark's christology.[188] However, because such honorific titles are valued in some cultures – such as the Turkish culture – they should be wisely and sensitively emphasised in contextualisation of the Good News for the people of such cultural milieus.

---

[187] "Markan Christology", op. cit., 470-471.

[188] Earl Johnson, op. cit., 16, wisely notes that – although all of the christological titles used, for example, in Mk. 15 – "come close to the truth in the context in which they are found or on the lips of those who speak them *they do not contain the full truth which the church needs to sustain its faith and follow Jesus*." [emphasis added].

6. CONCLUSIONS: IMPLICATIONS OF JESUS' AUTHORITY FOR MISSIOLOGY

If the veracity of the Markan account of Jesus' life and ministry is accepted, then it is a foregone conclusion that this authority figure constitutes a challenge to every human being and, thus, also has profound implications for all involved in gospel ministry. Specifically, Jesus – as presented in Mark's gospel – is one who should not only meet the Turks' felt need for an authoritative leader, who by virtue of his character, knowledge and power is the ideal and unique *üstat*[189], but will also meet their ultimate need of a saviour. It is proposed that God, in his amazing grace, allowed Turkish culture to develop with a marked appreciation for authority figures in anticipation of the proclamation of the ultimate spiritual *üstat*, Jesus. Moreover, if the Good News is to be properly and sensitively contextualised for Turkish culture, cross-cultural ministers should utilise this redemptive analogy *and* appropriately emphasise christological titles.

At the outset it was argued that sound missiology issues from sound theology. Mark's account is an historical narrative with a definite proclamatory intent; Mark was a believer who wanted to accurately communicate Jesus' person, teaching and work, and his gospel presents a preponderance of evidence that suggests that Jesus claimed *and* demonstrated unequalled authority. Furthermore, Jesus delegates his authority to his disciples in order that they carry on God's work of redemption. Consequently, an understanding *and* appropriation of Jesus' authority should guide our evangelism and discipleship – the latter as it affects our own personal spirituality *and* our training of others.

[189] Cf., Chapter 2, p. 12.

Evangelism

It has been established that at least one aspect of Mark's intent was kerygmatic; in other words, listeners or readers are challenged to respond *in faith* to the one presented.[190] The content of Mark's gospel, as we have seen, is the authoritative Jesus. As John Hitchen writes,

> Mark's Gospel narrative sets the foundation for an adequate understanding of the gospel. The features of the Good News outlined there *determine both the message we proclaim and the methods we adopt* in making it known.[191] [emphasis added]

In that Mark's account is clearly not a step-by-step evangelism-training manual, what might Hitchen be implying? He continues by summarising the new-life experience of the believer in transforming relationship with Christ via personal faith in Jesus Christ, and notes: "A valid experience of the gospel of Christ is all-embracing. He redirects the believers' life-styles and values systems."[192] It seems that Hitchen's point is that true discipleship is the key to evangelism. If we learn from Mark's account what discipleship demands, and live as authentic, committed disciples yielded to Jesus' authority in every area of life[193], we will consequently be equipped as evangelists and disciple-makers.

[190] Cf., Mk. 9:42 and 15:32.

[191] "Evangelism and Mission – What is the Gospel?," *SBET* 19/1 (2001): 28.

[192] Ibid., 29.

[193] John Kitchen's recent book, *Embracing Authority* (Fearn: CFP, 2002), helpfully sorts out many of the implications of authority, for mankind in general and for the Church in particular.

Discipleship

Many theologians have recognised that discipleship is a major theme or emphasis in Mark's theology.[194] It is also clear that the section of Mark that deals most profusely with discipleship is 8:22-10:52. R. T. France estimates that "some 35% of the teaching material in Mark [is] devoted fairly directly to the theory and practice of discipleship."[195]

First and foremost in Mark's account of discipleship is the aspect of *being called* into the master-disciple relationship. Joel Williams notes:

> Mark's Gospel has a rhetorical function. Mark did not write simply to convey historical information, theological ideas, or a well-formed story. Mark also wrote his Gospel *to move his readers to follow Jesus and live up to Jesus' demands. Mark's* Gospel is a call to discipleship. [196] (emphasis added)

Jesus does not want converts *per se* – he wants disciples. Mental assent is insufficient for, after all, "the demons believe – and shudder."[197] Schweizer's observation is trenchant: "Discipleship is the only form in which faith can exist."[198]

But what does it mean to be a disciple of Jesus and, according to Mark, what is the true nature of discipleship?[199] In so far as discipleship has to do with subscribing to the teachings and following the example of a master, being a disciple means having a leader.[200]

---

[194] E.g., Brooks, op. cit., 30; R. A. Guelich, "Gospel of Mark," in *Dictionary of Jesus and the Gospels*, eds. Joel B. Green and Scot McKnight (Downers Grove: IVP, 1992), 522-523; Evans, op. cit., 271-272; Edwards, *The Gospel according to Mark*, op. cit., 16; France, *The Gospel of Mark*, op. cit., 27-28.

[195] "Mark and the Teaching of Jesus," op. cit., 120.

[196] Op. cit., 335-336.

[197] James 2:19. See also Mk. 1:24 and 5:7.

[198] *The Good News*, op. cit., 386.

[199] Telford, *The Theology of the Gospel of Mark*, op. cit., 133, summarises Jesus' teaching concerning the marks of a true disciple: a disciple must be last of all and servant of all (Mk. 9:35); willing to take up his cross and follow Jesus (Mk. 8:34); must not seek to save his own life, but be willing to lose that life for Jesus' sake (Mk. 8:35); will not deny Jesus but confess him, and whoever is ashamed of Jesus will be denied by the Son of Man at his parousia (Mk. 8:38); he will also keep watch lest his master return and find him asleep (Mk. 13:35-37).

[200] Karl Heim, op. cit., 51, notes: "That the service of Christ excludes every other guidance of life is caused neither by the different content of His instructions as compared to all other programmes

Although we generally tend to favour leaders who are strong and successful, Schweizer points out that men throughout Mark's gospel reject Jesus, the ultimate leader. Nevertheless, men are called to follow him. Ironically, this leader "cannot be understood without his cross,"[201] and this understanding informs – and provides the contours of – discipleship.[202]

Thus, although Jesus is the perfectly authoritative leader – as indicated by his teaching and his mighty works – and therefore worthy of being trusted and followed, his own way ends with humiliation, torture and a cross; "all who follow Jesus on the 'way of the Lord' will be put to the test."[203] Just as it was necessary for Jesus to suffer, so do his followers.[204] This realisation is especially important in Turkey where evangelical national Christians number only 3500-4000 and regularly suffer or are discriminated against for their faith.[205] Consequently, Turks – and anyone else, for that matter – might be attracted to Jesus as one truly worthy of being followed, as one who not only claims but also demonstrates authority; however, true discipleship is only entered into after *having counted the cost*. France indicates that, in Mark, "emphasis is laid on the costly commitment involved, a cost which derives in part from the disciple's responsibility to engage in a mission to other men with the message of Jesus."[206] So discipleship *is* "Follow the Leader", but this is no schoolyard game; it promises "self-denial, sacrifice, and willing, humble service"[207] and,

---

of conduct, nor by the distinction between freedom and coercion. It simply follows from the character of guidance." That is, you can only have one lord – a single allegiance.

[201] "The Portrayal of the Life of Faith in the Gospel of Mark," *Int* 32/4 (1978): 389.

[202] E.g., Achtemeier, "'And He Followed Him': Miracles and Discipleship in Mark 10:46-52," *Semeia* 11/1 (1978): 136, posits: "Discipleship now means: following Jesus in the way of the cross."

[203] Susan Garrett, "Disciples on Trial," *ChrCent* 115 (1998): 398.

[204] Eg., Mk. 13:9-13, Jn. 15:18-25.

[205] Freedom of religion is guaranteed by Article 24 of the Turkish constitution but, practically speaking, that freedom has only been extended to the Muslim majority. That is, one is free to be a Muslim.

[206] "Mark and the Teaching of Jesus," op. cit., 119-120.

[207] Williams, op. cit., 343. So Guelich, op. cit., 523 and Evans op. cit., 272. Kingsbury, *Conflict in Mark*, op. cit., 104, argues that the essence of discipleship in Mark's account is servanthood.

possibly, the ultimate sacrifice.[208] Elizabeth Malbon comments concerning Christian discipleship: "...anyone can be a follower, no one finds it easy."[209] Consequently, "fear and disobedience are potential problems for any who choose to follow Jesus."[210]

Some might suggest that discipleship in Mark can be reduced to a *theologia crucis.* John Donahue, however, argues that "Discipleship is wider than imitation of Jesus' way of the cross and is grounded in the quest to seek and do the will of God."[211] He goes on to conclude that Mark's gospel targets not only those who have already believed, but also those who may be yet seeking.[212] Thus, Mark's message about Jesus is a call to obedience – unto believing faith for those still outside of Christ, and unto *faith-requiring, thoroughgoing imitation of Christ* for believers.[213] Jesus has delegated his own authority to all disciples in order to empower them to join him in his ministry of proclaiming the kingdom of God. Ernest Best observes:

> Though in the life of Jesus the cross and the resurrection were sequential, for the pilgrim [disciple] they are simultaneous; *mission and self-denial cannot ultimately be distinguished; cross-bearing and cross-proclaiming are opposite sides of the same coin.*[214] [emphasis added]

Therefore, proper imitation by the disciple includes not only the aspect of following Jesus in his character, suffering and humiliation, but also in his mission.[215]

Should Jesus be followed? Our foregoing survey of Mark's account strongly suggests that he should, for He claims and

---

[208] E.g., Achtemeier, "And He Followed Him," op. cit., 136, writes: "Mark clearly thinks of discipleship primarily in relation to the passion of Jesus."

[209] *In the Company of Jesus* (Louisville: WJK, 2000), 67.

[210] Joel F. Williams, *Other Followers of Jesus* (Sheffield: JSOT Press, 1994), 205.

[211] "A Neglected Factor in the Theology of Mark," *JBL* 101/4 (1982): 594.

[212] Ibid. This conclusion is germane to the earlier discussion (Ch. 4) of intent/genre. Thus Donahue argues that Mark's account intended to influence both the believing community and also those still outside of the kingdom of God.

[213] P. G. Davis, "Divine Agents, Mediators, and New Testament Christology," *JTS* 45 (1994): 490, posits that "the Christian life is *the Christ-like life, defined by the imitation of his threefold work* of ministering, suffering, and judging (3:14-15; 6:7-11; 13:9-13)." [emphasis added].

[214] *Following Jesus*, op. cit., 249.

demonstrates a peerless kind of authority, as his opponents well understood. R.T. France aptly notes: "discipleship is the proper outcome of a healthy christology."[216] And if we have a healthy christology, then we are well on the way toward sound theology and missiology.

[215] Anne Dawson, op. cit., 170, summarises the latter point well: "Mark's understanding of the concept of discipleship that Jesus espoused, was a radical transformation of the *praxis* of discipleship where inclusiveness in the mission of Jesus was the norm…".

[216] *The Gospel of Mark*, op. cit, 28.

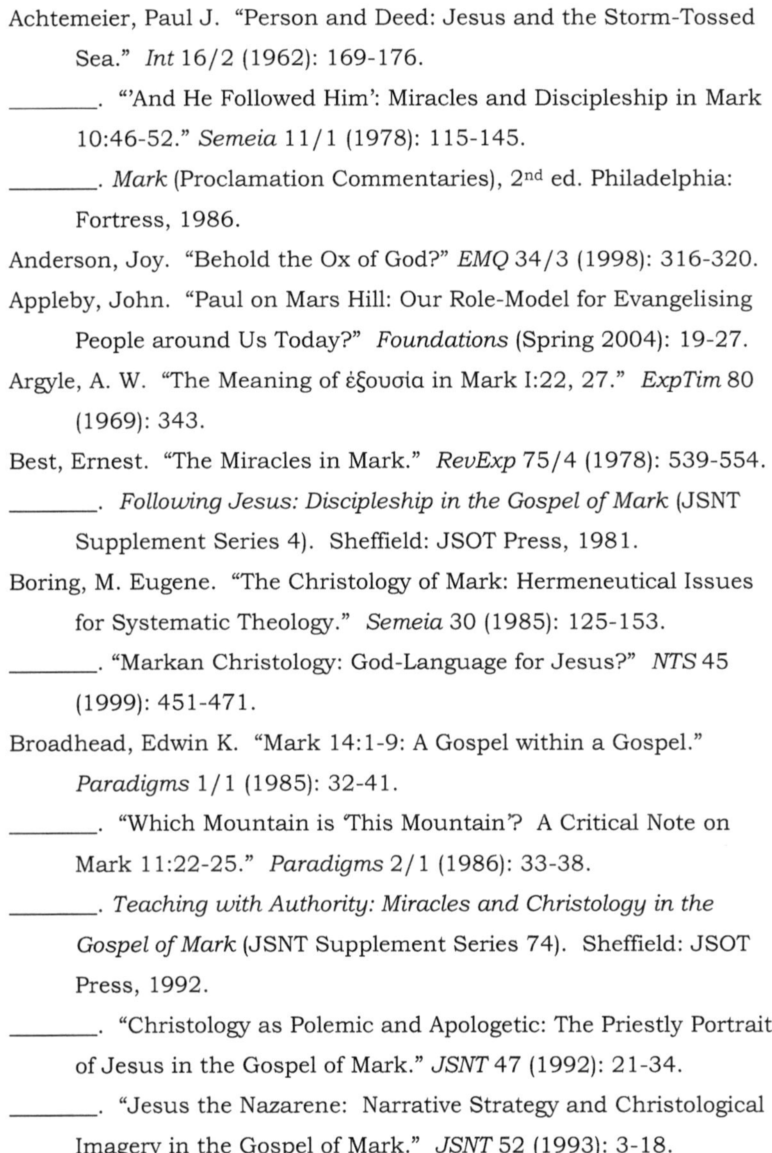

BIBLIOGRAPHY

Achtemeier, Paul J. "Person and Deed: Jesus and the Storm-Tossed Sea." *Int* 16/2 (1962): 169-176.

_______. "'And He Followed Him': Miracles and Discipleship in Mark 10:46-52." *Semeia* 11/1 (1978): 115-145.

_______. *Mark* (Proclamation Commentaries), 2nd ed. Philadelphia: Fortress, 1986.

Anderson, Joy. "Behold the Ox of God?" *EMQ* 34/3 (1998): 316-320.

Appleby, John. "Paul on Mars Hill: Our Role-Model for Evangelising People around Us Today?" *Foundations* (Spring 2004): 19-27.

Argyle, A. W. "The Meaning of ἐξουσία in Mark I:22, 27." *ExpTim* 80 (1969): 343.

Best, Ernest. "The Miracles in Mark." *RevExp* 75/4 (1978): 539-554.

_______. *Following Jesus: Discipleship in the Gospel of Mark* (JSNT Supplement Series 4). Sheffield: JSOT Press, 1981.

Boring, M. Eugene. "The Christology of Mark: Hermeneutical Issues for Systematic Theology." *Semeia* 30 (1985): 125-153.

_______. "Markan Christology: God-Language for Jesus?" *NTS* 45 (1999): 451-471.

Broadhead, Edwin K. "Mark 14:1-9: A Gospel within a Gospel." *Paradigms* 1/1 (1985): 32-41.

_______. "Which Mountain is 'This Mountain'? A Critical Note on Mark 11:22-25." *Paradigms* 2/1 (1986): 33-38.

_______. *Teaching with Authority: Miracles and Christology in the Gospel of Mark* (JSNT Supplement Series 74). Sheffield: JSOT Press, 1992.

_______. "Christology as Polemic and Apologetic: The Priestly Portrait of Jesus in the Gospel of Mark." *JSNT* 47 (1992): 21-34.

_______. "Jesus the Nazarene: Narrative Strategy and Christological Imagery in the Gospel of Mark." *JSNT* 52 (1993): 3-18.

_______. *Prophet, Son, Messiah: Narrative Form and Function in Mark 14-16* (JSNT Supplement Series 97). Sheffield: JSOT Press, 1994.

_______. "Form and Function in the Passion Story: The Issue of Genre Reconsidered." *JSNT* 61 (1996): 3-28.

_______. *Mark* (Readings: A New Biblical Commentary). Sheffield: SAP, 2001.

Broer, Ingo. "ἐξουσία." In *Exegetical Dictionary of the New Testament*, eds. Horst Balz & Gerhard Schneider, 9-12. Grand Rapids: Eerdmans, 1981 (Eng. 1991).

Brooks, James A. *Mark* (New American Commentary). Nashville: Broadman, 1991.

Bryan, Christopher. *A Preface to Mark: Notes on the Gospel in its Literary and Cultural Settings.* New York/Oxford: OUP, 1993.

Campbell-Jack, W. C. "Common Grace and Eschatology." *SBET* 7/2 (1989), 100-115.

Chouinard, Larry. "Gospel Christology: A Study of Methodology." *JSNT* 30 (1987): 21-37.

Collins, Adela Yarbro. *The Beginning of the Gospel: Probings of Mark in Context.* Eugene, Oregon*: Wipf and Stock Publishers, 2001 [Augsburg Fortress, 1992).

Corwin, Gary. "Reaching the Resistant." *EMQ* 34/2 (1998): 144-145.

Daube, David. "ἐξουσια in Mark I 22 and 27." *JTS* 39 (1938): 45-59.

Davis, Philip G. "Mark's Christological Paradox." *JSNT* 35 (1989): 3-18.

_______. "Divine Agents, Mediators, and New Testament Christology." *JTS* 45 (1994): 479-503.

Dawson, Anne. *Freedom as Liberating Power: A Socio-Political Reading of the* ἐξουσια *Texts in the Gospel of Mark* (Novum Testamentum et Orbis Antiquus 44). Göttingen: Vandenhoeck & Ruprecht, Universitatsverlag Freiburg Schweiz, 2000.

* In this bibliography, USA state names are only spelled out for less well-known cities/towns.

Dillon, Richard J. "'As One Having Authority' (Mark 1:22): The Controversial Distinction of Jesus' Teaching." *CBQ* 57/1 (2001): 92-113.

Donahue, John R. "A Neglected Factor in the Theology of Mark." *JBL* 101/4 (1982): 563-594.

Doughty, Darrell J. "The Authority of the Son of Man (Mk 2:1-3:6)." *ZNW* 74 (1983): 161-181.

Dowd, Sharyn. *Reading Mark: A Literary and Theological Commentary on the Second Gospel.* Macon, Georgia: Smith & Helwys, 2000.

Dwyer, Timothy. "The Motif of Wonder in the Gospel of Mark." *JSNT* 57 (1995): 49-59.

Edwards, James R. "Markan Sandwiches: The Significance of Interpolations in Markan Narratives." *NovT* 31/3 (1989): 193-216.

________. "The Baptism of Jesus according to the Gospel of Mark." *JETS* 34/1 (1991): 43-57.

________. "The Authority of Jesus in the Gospel of Mark." *JETS* 37/2 (1994): 217-233.

________. *The Gospel according to Mark* (Pillar NTC). Grand Rapids: Eerdmans, 2002.

Evans, C. A. "Mark." In *New Dictionary of Biblical Theology*, eds. T. Desmond Alexander and Brian S. Rosner, 267-273. Leicester: IVP, 2000.

Foerster, Werner. "ἐξουσία." In *Theological Dictionary of the New Testament.* Grand Rapids: Eerdmans, 1964-1976. 2:562-574.

France, R. T. "Mark and the Teaching of Jesus." In *Gospel Perspectives: Studies of History and Tradition in the Four Gospels*, Vol. 1, eds. R. T. France and David Wenham, 101-136. Sheffield: JSOT Press, 1980.

________. *Divine Government: God's Kingship in the Gospel of Mark.* London: SPCK, 1990.

_______. *The Gospel of Mark, A Commentary on the Greek Text* (NIGTC). Grand Rapids: Eerdmans, 2002.

Garrett, Susan R. *The Temptations of Jesus in Mark's Gospel.* Grand Rapids: Eerdmans, 1998.

_______. "Disciples on Trial." *ChrCent* 115 (1998): 396-399.

Gathercole, Simon J. "The Son of Man in Mark." *ExpTim* 115 (2004): 366-372.

Geldenhuys, Norval. *Supreme Authority: The Authority of the Lord, His Apostles and the New Testament.* London: Marshall, Morgan & Scott, 1953.

Glasson, T. Francis. "The Uniqueness of Christ: The New Testament Witness." *EvQ* 43/1 (1971): 25-35.

Guelich, R. A. "Gospel of Mark." In *Dictionary of Jesus and the Gospels*, eds. Joel B. Green and Scot McKnight, 512-525. Downers Grove: IVP, 1992.

Harrison, R. K. "The Son of Man." *EvQ* 23/1 (1951): 46-50.

Heim, Karl. *Jesus the Lord: The Sovereign Authority of Jesus and God's Revelation in Christ.* Edinburgh: Oliver & Boyd, 1959.

Hellerman, Joseph H. "Challenging the Authority of Jesus: Mark 11:27-33 and Mediterranean Notions of Honor and Shame." *JETS* 43/2 (2000): 213-228.

Hengel, Martin. *Studies in the Gospel of Mark.* London: SCM, 1985.

Herklots, H. G. G. *Not as the Scribes: A Study in the Authority of Jesus.* London: SCM, 1934.

Hesselgrave, David J., and Edward Rommen. *Contextualization: Meanings, Methods, and Models.* Grand Rapids: Baker, 1989.

Hitchen, John M. "Evangelism and Mission – What is the Gospel?" *SBET* 19/1 (2001): 4-30.

Hooker, Morna D. *The Son of Man in Mark: A Study of the Background of the Term "Son of Man" and its Use in St Mark's Gospel.* London: SPCK, 1967.

_______. *Studying the New Testament.* London: Epworth Press, 1979.

_______. “Mark.” In *It is Written: Scripture Citing Scripture – Essays in Honour of Barnabas Lindars, SSF*, eds. D. A. Carson & H. G. M. Williamson, 220-230. Cambridge: CUP, 1988.

_______. *The Gospel according to Saint Mark* (Black’s NT Commentaries). London: A. & C. Black, 1991.

Jackson, Howard M. “The Death of Jesus in Mark and the Miracle from the Cross.” *NTS* 33 (1987): 16-37.

Johnson, Earl S. “Is Mark 15:39 the Key to Mark’s Christology?” *JSNT* 31 (1987): 3-22.

Jones, James. *The Power and the Glory: The Authority of Jesus.* London: Darton, Longman & Todd, 1994.

Keck, Leander E. “Toward the Renewal of New Testament Christology.” *NTS* 32 (1986): 362-377.

Kee, Howard Clark. *Community of the New Age: Studies in Mark’s Gospel.* London: SCM, 1977.

Kennedy, George A. *New Testament Interpretation through Rhetorical Criticism.* Chapel Hill, North Carolina: UNC Press, 1984.

Kim, Seyoon. *The Son of Man as the Son of God.* Grand Rapids: Eerdmans, 1985 [1983].

Kim, Tae Hun. “The Anarthrous *υἱός θεοῦ* in Mark 15:39 and the Roman Imperial Cult.” *Bib* 79 (1998): 221-241.

Kingsbury, Jack Dean. “The ‘Divine Man’ as the Key to Mark’s Christology – The End of an Era?” *Int* 35/3 (1981): 246-257.

_______. *The Christology of Mark’s Gospel.* Philadelphia: Fortress, 1983.

_______. *Conflict in Mark: Jesus, Authorities, Disciples.* Minneapolis: Fortress, 1989.

_______. “The Religious Authorities in the Gospel of Mark.” *NTS* 36 (1990): 42-65.

Kitchen, John A. *Embracing Authority.* Fearn: CFP, 2002.

Lane, William L. *The Gospel according to Mark.* Grand Rapids: Eerdmans, 1974.

_______. "From Historian to Theologian: Milestones in Markan Scholarship." *RevExp* 75/4 (1978): 601-617.

Lemcio, Eugene E. "The Intention of the Evangelist, Mark." *NTS* 32 (1986): 187-206.

Lewis, Bernard. *What Went Wrong? The Clash between Islam and Modernity in the Middle East.* London: Weidenfeld & Nicolson, 2002.

Lewis, Peter. *The Glory of Christ.* Chicago: Moody Press, 1997.

Lindars, Barnabas. *Jesus, Son of Man: A Fresh Examination of the Son of Man Sayings in the Gospels.* Grand Rapids: Eerdmans, 1984 (London: SPCK, 1983).

Lloyd-Jones, D. Martyn. *Authority.* Edinburgh: BOT, 1992 (1958).

Lococo, Donald J. *Towards a Theology of Science.* Toronto: Novalis, 2002.

McDermott, Gerald R. *Can Evangelicals Learn from the World Religions? Jesus, Revelation & Religious Traditions.* Downers Grove: IVP, 2000.

McQuilkin, Robertson. *Understanding and Applying the Bible* (rev. ed.). Chicago: Moody, 1992 (1983).

Malbon, Elizabeth Struthers. *In the Company of Jesus: Characters in Mark's Gospel.* Louisville: WJK, 2000.

_______. *Hearing Mark: A Listener's Guide* Harrisburg, Pennsylvania: Trinity Press, 2002.

Marcus, Joel. "Mark 14:61: 'Are You the Messiah-Son-God?'" *NovT* 31/2 (1989): 125-141.

_______. *The Way of the Lord: Christological Exegesis of the Old Testament in the Gospel of Mark.* Edinburgh: T. & T. Clark, 1992.

Marshall, I. Howard. "The Divine Sonship of Jesus." *Int* 21/1 (1967): 87-103.

Martin, Ralph P. *Mark: Evangelist & Theologian.* Grand Rapids: Zondervan, 1973 [1972].

Matera, Frank J. "The Prologue as the Interpretive Key to Mark's Gospel." In *The Interpretation of Mark* (2nd ed.), ed. William Telford, 289-306. Edinburgh: T. & T. Clark, 1995.

Mawhinney, Allen. "Baptism, Servanthood, and Sonship." *WTJ* 49 (1987): 35-64.

Mittwede, Steven K. "Evangelism at Athens: Paul's Adaptability." *Reformation Today* 161 (1998): 15-18.

Myers, Ched, Marie Dennis, Joseph Nangle, Cynthia Moe-Lobeda, and Stuart Taylor. *'Say to this Mountain': Mark's Story of Discipleship.* Maryknoll, New York: Orbis, 1996.

Nicholls, Bruce J. *Contextualization: A Theology of Gospel and Culture.* Downers Grove: IVP, 1979.

Nineham, D. E. *The Gospel of St Mark* (Pelican Gospel Commentaries). Harmondsworth: Penguin, 1963.

Osborne, Grant R. "Structure and Christology in Mark 1:21-45." In *Jesus of Nazareth: Lord and Christ – Essays on the Historical Jesus and New Testament Christology*, eds. Joel B. Green and Max Turner, 147-163. Grand Rapids: Eerdmans, 1994.

Özdemir, Adil, and Kenneth Frank. *Visible Islam in Modern Turkey.* Basingstoke: Macmillan, 2000.

Öztürk, Yaşar Nuri. *The Eye of the Heart: An Introduction to Sufism and the Tariqats of Anatolia and the Balkans.* İstanbul: Redhouse, 1988.

Parshall, Phil. "Danger! New Directions in Contextualization (with Two Responses by John Travis and Dean S. Gilliland)." *EMQ* 34/4 (1998): 404-417.

Redhouse Yayınevi. *Çağdaş Türkçe-İngilizce Redhouse Sözlüğü* [Redhouse Contemporary Turkish-English Dictionary]. İstanbul: Redhouse Yayınevi, 1983.

Richardson, Don. *Peace Child.* Glendale, California: G/L Regal, 1974.

_______. "Redemptive Analogies." In *Evangelical Dictionary of World*

Missions, eds. A. Scott Moreau, Harold Netland and Charles Van Engen, 812-813. Grand Rapids: Baker, 2000.

Robbins, Vernon K. "Mark 1.14-20: An Interpretation at the Intersection of Jewish and Graeco-Roman Traditions." *NTS* 28 (1982): 220-236.

_______. *Jesus the Teacher: A Socio-Rhetorical Interpretation of Mark.* Philadelphia: Fortress, 1984.

Robertson, A. T. *Studies in Mark's Gospel* (revised and edited by Heber F. Peacock). Nashville: Broadman, 1958.

Robins, Philip. *Turkey and the Middle East.* London: Pinter/RIIA, 1991.

Sagovsky, Nicholas. "Lifelines: Church and Authority." *Anvil* 14/3 (1997): 207-210.

Schulz, Siegfried. "Mark's Significance for the Theology of Early Christianity." In *The Interpretation of Mark*, ed. William Telford, 158-166. London: SPCK, 1985.

Schweizer, Eduard. *The Good News according to Mark.* London: SPCK, 1971 [Knox, 1970].

_______. "The Portrayal of the Life of Faith in the Gospel of Mark." *Int* 32/4 (1978): 387-399.

Sire, James W. *The Universe Next Door: A Basic Worldview Catalog* (3rd ed.). Downers Grove: IVP, 1997.

Speers, John. "Ramadan: Should Missionaries keep the Muslim Fast?" *EMQ* 27/4 (1991): 356-359.

Tannehill, Robert C. "The Gospel of Mark as Narrative Christology." *Semeia* 16/1 (1979): 57-95.

Telford, William, ed. *The Interpretation of Mark.* London: SPCK, 1985.

_______. *The Theology of the Gospel of Mark.* Cambridge: CUP, 1999.

Tiessen, Terrance L. *Who Can be Saved?: Reassessing Salvation in Christ and World Religions.* Downers Grove: IVP, 2004.

Tolbert, Mary Ann. *Sowing the Gospel: Mark's World in Literary-Historical Perspective.* Minneapolis: Fortress, 1989.

Trakatellis, Demetrios. *Authority and Passion: Christological Aspects of the Gospel according to Mark*. Brookline, Massachusetts: Holy Cross Orthodox Press, 1987.

Ulansey, David. "The Heavenly Veil Torn: Mark's Cosmic 'Inclusio'." *JBL* 110/1 (1991): 123-125.

Vorster, W. S. "Kerygma/History and the Gospel Genre." *NTS* 29 (1983): 87-95.

Wakely, Mike. "The Search for the Golden Key." *EMQ* 40/1 (2004): 12-22.

Weeden, T. J. "The Heresy that Necessitated Mark's Gospel," *ZNW* 59 (1968): 145-158.

Westerholm, Stephen. *Jesus and Scribal Authority* (Coniectanea Biblica, NT Series 10). Lund: CWK Gleerup, 1978.

Williams, Joel F. *Other Followers of Jesus: Minor Characters as Major Figures in Mark's Gospel* (JSNT Supplement Series 102). Sheffield: JSOT Press, 1994.

_______. "Discipleship and Minor Characters in Mark's Gospel." *BSac* 153 (1996): 332-343.

Woods, Scott. "Biblical Look at C5 Muslim Evangelism." *EMQ* 39/2 (2003): 188-195.

Yörükhân, Yusuf Ziya. *Müslümanlık ve Kur'an-ı Kerim'den Âyetlerle İslâm Esasları* (Islam and its Essentials, with Qur'anic Proofs) [Cultural Works Series No. 222]. Ankara: Turkish Ministry of Culture, 2002.

Zeller, Dieter. "New Testament Christology in its Hellenistic Reception." *NTS* 46 (2001): 312-333.

APPENDIX 1. On Revelation and Its Authority

Subjective "believerism" – reflected in comments such as "Don't try to confuse me with facts!" – is a dangerous position for anyone involved in serious academic enquiry. However, possession of unwavering theological commitments does not necessarily violate aspirations to something that approximates objectivity. All researchers have presuppositions with which they approach their subject matter in the pursuit of truth-seeking. After all, even those who reject the concept of absolute truth embrace that position as an absolute.

In the interest of academic integrity, I present my position on the revelation of Scripture and its authority by quoting Roman Catholic scientist-theologian Donald Lococo:

> Revelation is a definitive authority for theology because it is God's truth...The strength of the argument from authority is proportionate to the credibility of the claimant. Whereas human authority is always finite and fallible, divine authority is infinite and infallible. If the authority is the infinitely transcendent God, then the veracity of the source and the truth revealed cannot be in question. To eliminate the possibility of a divine authority would require a greater authority than the one dismissed. A truth spoken by a scientific authority *can* be discovered to be true through reason. Revelation, by contrast, can never become a possession of reason; it cannot be turned into an insight of our own.[217]

This is not to say that faith commitments are unreasonable. If an individual begins to sense that his previously held worldview does not satisfactorily answer the ultimate questions of life, he will become restless and seek a new belief system that does. I submit that the most satisfying answers are available to that person in divine revelation.[218] If allowed, revelation and reason will operate synergistically, yet never does revelation become the slave of human reason. In the words of Pascal, "The supreme achievement of reason is to bring us to see that there is a limit to reason."[219]

---

[217] *Towards a Theology of Science* (Toronto: Novalis, 2002): 40-41.

[218] This is not to suggest that all truth is metaphysical. However, all truth *is* God's truth. As James Sire notes, "A worldview satisfies by being true…[and] truth is ultimately the only thing that will satisfy." *The Universe Next Door*, 3rd ed. (Downers Grove: IVP, 1997), 198.

[219] Quoted in Lloyd-Jones, op. cit., 13.

Printed by Books on Demand GmbH, Norderstedt / Germany